CALL ME CHARLIE

CHARLIE NIRENBERG

Founder and Chairman,
Dairy Mart

Copyright, 1992, Charles Nirenberg, Enfield, Connecticut

First Edition Published, 1992, by Convenient Publishing Company, Enfield, Connecticut

Jacket Design by Rob LaChance of Tin Can Alley and Denis Connors of Curran & Connors.

The Jimmy Fund

ONE OF THE nice things about this book is that we can help fight cancer through research. All the profits go to the Jimmy Fund of the Dana-Farber Cancer Institute.

Here is an excerpt from the Dana-Farber magazine, "Paths of Progress," WESTWARD HO!

Thanks to Dairy Mart's Charles Nirenberg, the Jimmy Fund isn't just New England's charity

When it comes to Dana-Farber's Jimmy Fund, Charles Nirenberg likes to think big—as big as the whole U.S.A. The founder and CEO of Dairy Mart Convenience Stores wants everyone in America to know that the Jimmy fund is helping save lives. And he wants them to give.

The man who got his start behind the wheel of an ice cream truck is bringing word of New England's favorite charity to customers at nearly 1,200 stores in Indiana, Ohio, Michigan, Pennsylvania, Tennessee, North Carolina and Kentucky, as well as Connecticut, Massachusetts, New York and Rhode Island. By the fall of 1991, store patrons had boosted Dairy Mart's total contributions to the Jimmy Fund to $1 million.

"Cancer is not just a New England disease," says Nirenberg, who, with his wife, Jan, also has lent generous personal support to the Jimmy Fund.

"Given that research pioneered at the Institute saves lives

throughout the world, there's every reason for every American to support the Jimmy Fund."

Nirenberg, a member of Dana-Farber's Board of Overseers, may be a seasoned businessman—to TV viewers who have seen his trademark commercials, Nirenberg is Dairy Mart—but he's watching more than the bottom line. The day in 1987 that the stockmarket collapsed was one he will never forget. "I had spent the day at Dana-Farber, taping a video to inform our employees about the Institute's patients and programs," he says, "That experience—talking with doctors, seeing the children—helped put the crash, bad as it was, into perspective."

"For years, Dairy Mart has been promoting the Jimmy Fund right alongside milk and eggs," notes Nirenberg. Stores run special promotions and fundraisers, with incentives for managers to raise money. Coin canisters are posted beside cash registers. Golf tournaments are held annually in Ohio, Kentucky and New England. Last year, Nirenberg filmed TV spots with comedian Norm Crosby and the Baseball Hall of Fame's Carl Yastrzemski that underscored Dairy Mart's commitment to the Jimmy Fund.

Dairy Mart aims to double its $1 million donation within three years, Nirenberg says. Small wonder the company's success is mirrored in its crowd-pleasing credo: "Good People . . . it must be Dairy Mart."

> Charlie Nirenberg's support of the Jimmy Fund has been absolutely outstanding and an inspiration to everyone connected with our work. There has to be a special place in everyone's heart for Charlie.
>
> —Mike Andrews,
> Executive Director,
> The Jimmy Fund

Dedication

THIS IS A story in which I tell about my mother's generation and my own generation, but more important is the generation we made possible—that of my grandchildren. That's why this book is dedicated to them:

JOSHUA MURRAY
JILLIANN RACHEL
JAMES PHELPS
MADELEINE SARAH

and any others who may come along.

Thank You

RIGHT IN THE beginning of this book I would like to acknowledge the help I have gotten from many people who contributed time, energy and thought to making this book possible:

They include the staff at Dairy Mart especially Noreen Forbes, Cindy Bovat and Tina Doran. Rob LaChance and Denis Connors have given of their creative talents including the jacket. My colleagues Frank Colaccino, Ford Goldman, Mitch Kupperman, and Jerry Hassett have added their ideas. My daughters Sandi and Pam, agent Natashia Kern, have contributed their guidance and support. And, of course, none of it would have happened without my wife, Jan.

Charlie Nirenberg
Enfield, Connecticut
1992

Tribute to George Mair

GHOST WRITERS ARE usually not revealed and kept in the genie bottle. Well, I'm letting the genie out of the bottle. There is no way that I can allow this book to be published without paying tribute to George Mair, who was my ghost writer.

He has a way of telling a story that is very unique. Some who have read the manuscript have said that they can really hear me talking, so I think, George, you have been able to capture me. He has added the emotion, the pain, the excitement, and the exhilaration to my life story so that one can really get to know me.

Let me tell you who George Mair really is. Educated and raised in California, he has been a teacher and soldier, builder and banker, CBS broadcaster and L.A. TIMES nationally syndicated columnist, chief press officer to the Speaker of Congress and a radio talk-show host.

He studied business and economics at UCLA where he became assistant to the Dean of Students and, then, aide-de-camp to Maj. Gen. F. C. Holbrook during the Korean War. He ran the family building/banking business for 10 years—teaching and writing on business part-time. He became Editorial Director at CBS Radio in 1967. He wrote/produced 3,000+ editorials, 100 documentaries and won 32 awards.

He moved to Washington, D.C. as a *L.A. TIMES* nationally syndicated columnist. He became editor-publisher of America's oldest daily newspaper, the Alexandria *GAZETTE*, in

1982. He became Chief Public Relations Counsel for HBO/TIME, Inc. in 1985.

He returned to Washington in 1987, finished his 10th book, became Press Officer to the Speaker of Congress. He left federal service mid-1989 to be a talk show host on radio station WPGC.

He has traveled around the world visiting 21 countries from Ireland to Denmark to Israel to Kenya to Nepal to Australia to Japan and the Canadian Arctic. His books have been favorably reviewed in *"The New York Review of Books,"* the *"Los Angeles Times,"* and *"Publisher's Weekly."*

Call Me Charlie

A FEW WORDS UP FRONT . . .

This is a story I never thought I would tell anybody. It is the story of a bone-poor kid from Millis, Massachusetts, who lived the American dream and made it come true.

My reason for telling the story is to share some of the private things in my life with you. Perhaps you will find an idea you like or find helpful or, at least, entertaining.

For openers, let me say no life happens in a vacuum.

What any of us is or accomplishes has a lot to do with many other people—some of whom we never meet and some of whom we don't even know. In my case, for example, the mere fact that I am alive may be due to the momentary kindness or mercy of an unknown mounted Cossack with his long winter coat, fur hat, and saber, or a Communist soldier who didn't murder my mother while she was trapped in the little Ukrainian village of Koretz, where she waited for ten years until my father was able to send for her and their children.

Far fetched? Not really. Between the anti-Semitic pogroms of the Russian Czars, the battles of World War I and the devastating Russian Civil War with the rival Red and White Communist armies raging across the Ukrainian countryside, many Jews were massacred. There were 6,000 Jews living in Koretz, Ukraine, on the drizzly morning my tailor father began walking on his 7,000 mile journey westward to America, with a bolt of cloth, scissors, needle and thread. After World War II, there were exactly two Jews left alive in Koretz—neither of them were Nirenbergs.

My success is partially due to Henry Ford, an anti-Semitic industrialist whom I never met, and who invented the Flivver and the Tin Lizzie. And, it's partly due to Jodie Thompson, Jr., who made $2,300 in the summer of 1924 selling ice cold watermelons from an ice-house dock in Oak Cliff, Texas. You will see how what these and other men did changed the face of America and shaped my life and career.

To give my story a richer perspective than I can provide by myself, I have asked others who have touched my life to draw from their palettes to enrich and fill out the portrait.

CHAPTER I

Two Days Etched in My Memory

I KNEW SHE would die, but I never knew what would happen inside me as I stood by her grave.

It was in the West Roxbury Jewish Cemetery, which is arranged according to each village in Russia from which the occupants originally came. I was 49 years old, standing in the Koretz section by mother's marker and thinking about the irony of my mother's death.

One of the happiest days of my life had been only six weeks before. I had finally proven to my mother that all her struggles were worth it. We went to visit her in the nursing home in Springfield four or five times a week, and that day I had the joy of telling her that I had become a multi-millionaire! Her little boy who had sold eggs in front of the old Millis farmhouse was still selling eggs, but had made millions of dollars doing it. He had come a long way.

Now, as if my achievement was her final fulfillment and the family had security, money and safety so there was nothing left requiring her attention, she died.

Even so, that life force connection and energy was and will always be with me. When she died, it was hard to explain what was going on inside me. No matter what happened, she is still with me.

2   CALL ME CHARLIE

He adored her. He idolized her. She was the smartest, the most wonderful, the most giving person that he will ever meet in his life. He admired her brilliance. He admired her ability to—no matter what—find a way to make things work out. He went to her for advice. There was something about the way she told him things that he was always amazed and listened to her.

—My Daughter Sandi

They all came to the funeral—the family, friends, and all those rich and important executives from the Giant Corporation who had made me a millionaire a few weeks before. These powerful men from the rarified atmosphere of high corporate finance came to pay their respects to my mother—a tailor's wife from the Ukraine.

How proud she would be of her family and of me. We had made it. The Nirenbergs were people of position, and important men came in their dark suits, meticulous haircuts, and big chauffeur-driven cars to stand with heads bowed to do honor to my mother. My mother, who had endured humiliation, hardship, hunger, fear, and danger to nurture her children. Now we were no longer poor ice cream peddlers. Now, we were no longer outcast Jews.

It was as if my entire life suddenly came down to a single coherent, illuminated meaning. The one human being in the world with whom I had the longest mystical, energizing bond was gone. When a part of your psyche is taken, you reflect on your life and what it has been and what it will be in time to come. That may be why I wanted to write all this down.

The death of my mother—my children called her Bubbe, an affectionate word for grandmother—made me dwell on what she had been in my life and the many times when she had been there for me and I for her. Particularly the day of the red wagon and the fire.

Before I was born, she had pushed my father, who was now lying in the ground beside her, to make a courageous and difficult journey to America so he could then bring her, my two brothers, and my sister to a new, happier life. She waited and struggled to survive for ten years—ten very important years when you are in your twenties—through a World War, a revolution, and a civil war, until father was able to send for her.

Then, she made a home for all six of us—I was born in the second year after she finally came to America—in a three-room flat on Boston's Harrison Avenue.

With the money she made, our family was able to buy a ten-acre farm 20 miles outside of town in the community of Millis, where I grew up and began to know my mother and my family. My father was gone much of the time, so my mother was the central figure in the family. That would have been true even if my father had been around all the time. Mother was the strong one for all of us.

The Millis place was a modest house with brown shingles and a pebble driveway set back from the road with a chicken coop out in the back. It sat on an incredible ten acres of land which, in itself, was a pretty amazing thing for an immigrant family that had only been in this country for a couple of years.

Nobody talked about it, but the reason we could afford to buy this farm or to survive at all was because my mother and I were bootleggers—except I didn't know it.

She built a small still in our apartment to make illegal booze, which she then put into half-pint bottles and concealed under the mattress of my baby carriage. She was a booze pushcart lady, and I was her partner. The money for the downpayment and most of the monthly payments on the old Millis farm came from this trade of my mother's.

> *The interesting part wasn't that she sold booze. It was why she did it and what she was willing to do for her family. Charlie learned that you have to help your family and do what's necessary and help the people in the companies you're involved in to grow and develop. That's the story inside the story of his mother's bootlegging.*
> —My son-in-law, Mitch Kupperman

I remember it as one of those joyful days in a kid's life at our farm house.

I was just a boy who had turned five living with my family, and I'll never forget that birthday. My older brothers and sister got me a prized red wagon. I was too young to realize that we were poor, but I knew I had never had such a present and it was the most wonderful gift in the world.

I played with that wagon all day long—pulling it, riding in it while someone pulled me around the yard, taking it with me into the limitless world of a child's imagination, pretending it was a big red fire truck or just sitting in it alone relishing the luxury of my own red wagon. After a time, it grew dark and my older brothers and sister went to visit friends. My father, a tailor working in a crowded sewing room in Boston, wasn't home yet.

My mother and I were alone with the baby as we often were. It may have been this age differential that drew my mother and I so close together in those years as I grew up. The other children were older and off on their own, my father had a drinking problem and worked long hours so he wasn't around much, and there was just me and mother to take care of ourselves and the baby.

That's how it was December 13, 1928—the night of the red wagon. I was sitting there alone with her about 7 o'clock watching her feed the baby when it happened. All the lights went out.

In the darkness behind Mother, something terrifying loomed: dancing flames stretching upward, clawing at the ceiling. A ripple of cold fear swept through me as I cried out and pointed to the menacing fire devouring the back of our modest home.

With the assurance of action that characterized my mother all her life, she stood up quickly, grasping my baby brother, Joe, to her breast, and did what she would always do for me. She reached out a comforting, guiding hand and muttered reassuring words in Yiddish. I grasped her hand, as I would many times again both physically and psychologically, and she led me out of the flaming house. I probably was so scared that I squeezed her hand tight enough to hurt, but she made no complaint.

As we came out our front door, I could hear the consuming crackle of the flames behind us, and the smoke began curling into my nostrils. That's when the enormity of the tragedy happening before my eyes came crashing in on me. I looked back anxiously while mother pulled me onward. My wagon. My red wagon was gone and our house was engulfed in fire. I began to cry and press against my mother's leg to feel the comfort of her dress and her warm body as the one secure thing in an insecure world.

It meant nothing in particular to me at the time, but just as we emerged from the house, the police chief of Millis came rushing up to help by trying to take charge of me for my mother. He had seen the flames as he was coincidentally driving by.

He tried to take me away from the danger by grasping my free hand. I was having none of it. Nobody was going to take me away from my mother. She was the center of my universe. She was my rock. Looking back more than sixty years later, I realize that never changed in my entire life.

Soon the men came and they had a red wagon, too, except it was a grown-up red wagon used to put out fires. The men scurried all around with hoses and tools and finally subdued the searing flames.

My father came home from his job and he ran to embrace my mother as we all stared at what had once been our modest home. He cried and my mother cried and I cried and my brother cried.

> *He adored his mother and would do anything to ensure her well-being. My Bubbe was a character.*
>
> *You know, having a Bubbe that didn't speak English and looked very European with the funny black shoes with the laces, the hair in a bun, and, the nylons that she put a little knot in and shoved it down. It was embarrassing to me.*
>
> *But, as I got older, I began to realize just what Bubbe had to offer us. I think it was then that I realized what a wonderful woman she was and though she didn't know she looked different than other people, I thought, "I'm really lucky to have her."*
>
> —My Daughter Pam

The Maels, who lived across the road, were immediately outside in the night watching the fire and seeing what they could do to help. They insisted on the spot that we come into their home and stay there until our blackened, smoking house could be repaired.

During the weeks that followed, I spent every day watching the men rebuild our home from the blackened, charred ruin it had become that night. The smell. That's something I will never forget, the smell. After the firemen came and put out the flames amid the water-driven hissing, there was that smell of wet, scorched wood. It has been in all our nostrils at one time or another, but it stayed with me for a long, long time.

The other thing I remember is the Maels. They took us in and gave us a place to stay and food to eat. We stayed crowded with them in their house until ours could be re-occupied. They were so kind, and I wonder if people still do things like that for each other. I think they do, but I will never forget the kindness of those people who gave us shelter that frightening night.

In many ways our world had crumbled before our eyes, but one thing was always solid, safe, and soothing: my mother.

She was a mother driven by the vision of her family's safety and happiness. She was the presence in my life even when she wasn't there, because I was more a part of her than any of her children. I felt safe to venture, safe to dare, because I knew that, somewhere, she was always there to be my rudder in deep water.

She was a beautiful woman to me, with hair that reached down to the back of her knees. We never got to see all the hair. Later, my children kept spying on her to get a glimpse of it and finally did see it. Every morning she washed it, braided it, and rolled it into a bun before going into the kitchen and firing up the big, black cast iron stove so she could get her baking done. We all grew up depending on her.

And in turn she came to depend on me in ways she could not depend on others—least of all her husband. The greatest risk her husband ever took for her was getting them to America, and that seemed to exhaust him emotionally and brought him to the bottle.

It was my mother who held the family together during those ten lonely and dangerous years in Koretz while they waited for word from America. It was my mother who did what had to be done to support the family once it was in Massachusetts. If it took working every waking minute, she did it. If it took breaking the law and risking jail, she did it.

The first time I was old enough to understand our special bond was the day of the red wagon and the night of the fire. As it would be for years to come, I sensed it was just my mother and me with the baby.

These are very private thoughts, but I know now that they deserve to be known to my family and my friends and, in a way, to myself out loud. Putting them down here is a form of memorial to a courageous, loving woman who gave me life—nurtured and guided me. This story is a tribute to her.

CHAPTER II

The Promise and the Danger

THE DAY THE letter came to the town of Koretz huddled desperately against the Ukrainian countryside it set two young people on a road lined with danger, heartache, loneliness and hardship. I am a rich man today because they had the courage to take that road.

Getting the letter from America was dangerous. It had to pass through the hands of many who were not sympathetic to my people. They included agents of the Czar's secret police, who undoubtedly knew that a letter from America was delivered to the household of Louis Nirenberg, the master tailor, and his wife.

My mother Sarah could hardly wait until Louis came home from his 12-hour day tailoring so she could know what was in the letter from his brother Charles. It wasn't appropriate for her to open the letter. When Louis finally did arrive in their modest living quarters, she gave him the letter with a tremble inside her heart. Somehow she knew that it contained important news—of what, she wasn't sure—but they hadn't heard from Charles in over a year, so it must be important that he was writing now.

In the darkened room illuminated only a flickering lamp that gave off both light and the penetrating smell of kerosene, there was excitement as my father studied the outside of the envelope that had crossed an ocean and a continent to come to his hands.

My mother, an energetic, pragmatic woman born 50 years too soon, waited impatiently until her young husband finally ripped open the flap and used two fingers to fish out the folded paper nestled inside, with its tales of a magical land far from the beatings and oppression of Russia.

The handwriting was that of my Uncle Charles Nirenberg, who had seized a chance to leave Koretz three years before to make his way to Boston, Massachusetts, America. It had been a struggle, but Louis' brother Charles had gotten work through friends in a tailoring shop, and now there was room for another tailor. He wrote asking Louis to come to the land of opportunity, to come to America and join him. For Louis this was a troubling and dangerous invitation.

"What is it?" my mother probably asked to pull the news out of her reluctant husband.

"It's Charles. He wants me to join him in America." He gave voice to the hope that had buoyed my mother all day since the letter's arrival. For her, the courageous, adventurous one, it was a golden opportunity to escape the oppression of the Pale of Settlement.*

Under the present Russian system, her sons might be drafted into the Russian Army at age twelve for 35 years, forced to eat pork and converted into Christians against their will. That was the Czar's policy.

Mother didn't know how, but she knew that the America from which Charles was writing was different than the Russia in which she was now forced to live.

In America, horse-drawn carriages mixed uncomfortably on the dirt roads with the new-fangled motorcar. Most of the people of the country lived on farms. Electricity was the new miracle, people were experimenting with crude airplanes, and the radio was being developed. Primitive, jerky, black-and-white Nickelodeon movies began in some cities in 1905 and, three years later, there were 10,000 all around the country.

---

* 25 provinces centered on Kiev reaching south to the Black Sea in which Jews were forced to live from 1835 to 1917.

The Gibson Girl became the fashion ideal, with her hair piled on her head, pinched-in waist, a dreamy arrogant air on her face circling her Cupid's bow lips, and a skirt whose hemline had breathlessly risen to the daring height of the ankle. And hats. Everybody wore a hat, be it a derby or cap in the winter and straw boater in the summer for men, or the picture hat favored by the ladies.

Back in the small [shtible] house shared by the Nirenbergs in Koretz, the light from the lamp seemed to dip as my father probably heaved a sad sigh over the enormous problem his brother had sent into his home.

"Sarah, this is not easy. We have a good life here, with good work and good people. There are many obstacles. It is . . ."

Surely, it was at moments like these that Louis wondered why he married such a strong woman. He loved her from the moment they had met, while he was attending the school where her father taught. She was beautiful and more independent than a girl should be, and he knew he could never resist her even though, at 18, she was past the age when most girls married in their settlement.

Louis thought the very things about her that he admired were also the warning signs that this was no ordinary, subservient wife who would cook, scrub, and have babies. She used to lay on the floor outside the schoolroom and listen at the door to learn what the boys were learning, because girls were not allowed in the classroom. To have a wife who could read and talk of things she had learned from her father's books and that only men should know was something of which he was both proud and embarrassed.

In truth, she had conformed to much of what was expected of her as a devoted wife, even though there were moments when she clearly would have her way no matter what. In the past, those moments had been endurable. Now, as the couple lay down in bed to sleep, Louis faced the most serious of those moments in his life.

They talked on and on in the dark, as the children slept nearby in the same cold room, about the offer from Boston. For Sarah it meant escape. For Louis it meant danger. He would have to get permission to leave Koretz, but the Russian authorities might not let a skilled artisan leave.

Louis had grown up in this society and adjusted to it. He had a clean, warm job inside as a master tailor and only worked 12 hours a day, six days a week. He was better off than most, and now his wife wanted him to make a perilous journey to an unknown place thousands of miles away. It was crazy.

My mother was vitalized by the thought of getting to the freedom and riches of America. She weighed what was involved. First, they had to get Louis beyond the reach of the Russian authorities. If they could get Louis away, then he could send for Sarah and the three children in two, maybe three years, just as brother Charlie had sent for him.

To her, the alternative was perpetual oppression and poverty, under a regime that might loose a pogrom at any time and let the Army stand by idly as Sarah and Louis' people were looted, raped, and murdered.

And, so, reluctantly, it was settled. The next day my father went to the tailor room at his work with an apprehensive heart and a sealed tongue.

There had been money put away in a secret cache in their little nest, as Sarah's mother had cautioned her must be done against an uncertain future. Now this was the treasure that would give wings to her hopes and pay to take Louis to America. Because she could read the Russian newspaper in Koretz, Sarah knew of a German ship that would give Louis a bed and two meals a day when it sailed from Hamburg to New York City. It cost $79—more than a year's pay in Koretz.

For a Jew to be outside his village or outside the Pale without papers was forbidden. So Sarah, in her heavy peasant dress, laced black shoes, and babuska, trailing the bewildered children who clung to her skirt, walked to the office of the local magistrate.

She waited and she waited as the children shifted uncomfortably and her stomach complained for food. It meant nothing that a Jewess be kept waiting or be in discomfort while the greasy-bearded, sneering magistrate lorded it over all supplicants at his feet—particularly Jews.

When her time came to plead for his benefaction, she did what she would do all her life—anything that was necessary for her children. She stood in the crowded hearing room that smelled of unbathed bodies with her children around her, faced the Commissionaire with the heavy beard parted at the chin and the dark blue coat with the double row of brass buttons, and pled her cause. My mother needed a piece of paper from this petty tyrant. A piece of paper that would be a key to freedom. For that piece of paper she would have paid whatever she had. She would have kissed his feet.

As it was, all she had to do was humble herself, beg his help and tell him a lie he would accept. It has always been the tool of the oppressed to know the art of the believable lie. She said Louis needed to visit his sick brother in Warsaw and pled for the magistrate's noble permission for Louis to make the journey. Suspicious that he was being hoodwinked, as indeed he was, the sullen magistrate demanded to know why Louis was not before him on bended knee pleading his own cause.

Sarah, a woman who understood human nature and what was required, humbly explained that Louis was a master tailor and so devoted to the glorious Czar of all the Russias that he would not take a minute away from his service to that ruler simply for his own needs.

The petition was granted, and the precious piece of paper with the appropriate red sealing wax imprints, ribbons, and scrawled signatures was issued. This critical achievement was, of course, only the first step of a dangerous journey. Now Louis had to walk to Poland, pass beyond the boundary of The Pale, and continue until he reached the German port city of Hamburg. It would take many days and many nights.

It was dark when my father began his epic trek to the west. Mother had bundled him against the cold and filled his pockets with bread and cheese to sustain him. He was leaving Koretz, but he was taking his livelihood with him: a bolt of cloth, a pair of scissors, and a spool of thread in his pocket with a needle stuck into his coat lapel.

Koretz was barely stirring as the first rays of the eastern sun brightened the sky and Louis Nirenberg took the steps that would mean so much to his Sarah and their three children in years to come. And, to me, even though I was yet to be born.

He didn't dare show it when he embraced Sarah and said a grim good-bye, but they both knew that they might never see each other again, and that Louis might never reach the land of promise. Louis was secretly very afraid, but he would do what he had to do. It was a gamble that Sarah was willing to make and one that Louis had to make because Sarah wouldn't have it any other way.

Every morning for the next ten days, Louis rose before the sun and, eating a little of the bread or whatever he had been able to scrounge the day before, set his face westward with the warming sun on his back. At night, he would try to find a barn or a haystack or, lacking that, a field by the road where he could lay down and sleep the fitful sleep of a frightened and troubled man.

As he trudged on, he endured dust and then rain and mud. Once, near a small town where he asked directions, a Czarist policeman in a long, dark coat, with a fur hat on which was pinned the Imperial Czarist seal, demanded his papers. He carefully pulled the precious official paper from inside his clothes and showed it to the policeman who studied it and begrudgingly let him go on to the next town. It was highly probable that the policeman could not read what the official paper said but recognized the red wax seals and ribbons as something important and official.

Asking directions to the next town was how Louis made it to Warsaw. He had no map, only a list of the towns between Koretz and Warsaw that a friend had given him. In each town, he would ask the way to the next town on the list. That brought him, ten foot-sore days later, to the capital of Poland.

Here he sought out help from Jews in the community. He asked for the way west to Hamburg and was directed to a train station. Soon he was on his way to Hamburg. He found the shipping line, bought his ticket with the precious money he had left, and, three days later, sailed with the hopes and dreams of the Nirenberg family. He slept on a bed of hay in the hold of a cattle boat, along with 200 other emigrants.

Breakfast—one of the two meals included in the fare—was a course gruel, and supper was a nondescript stew of indeterminable ingredients. The trick was to close your eyes, not inhale the smell, and down it quickly.

> *There are things that I resented about my father and times when I was disappointed in him. Yet, I do remember that*

what he did for Sarah and the family in 1912 did take enormous courage.

Football coach Knute Rockne once spoke of courage. He said "courage means to be afraid to do something and still going ahead and do it. If a man has character, the right kind of energy, mental ability, he will learn that fear is something to overcome and not to run away from."

I think my father knew that and overcame his fears so that all of us could live a better life. I thank him for that.

One afternoon a great shout went up from some of the other passengers who were up forward. It brought everyone crowding toward the bow.

"There she is. We are here. It is America!" The deck was filled with the babble of many languages and a universal joy and relief, as some people jumped up and down with excitement and others began to dance and sing from happiness.

Before them was the enormous statue of a woman, towering above Ellis Island in New York Harbor, with a torch lifted high in one hand and a tablet grasped to her bosom in the other.

More of the tired, huddled masses yearning to be free had arrived, and Louis Nirenberg was among them.

CHAPTER III

Reaching a Strange New Land Just in Time

MY FATHER LOUIS was one of those who fled in 1912—just in time. Because of a dispute between the United States and Russia, it soon became harder for Jews to leave Russia. Between 1880 and 1914, 2,000,000 Russian Jews came to the United States, which finally began alarming American political conservatives in some quarters.

The America he found when he arrived at Ellis Island was in the process of dramatic changes that would alter the face of the nation forever. He was part of a flood of some 14 million immigrants who poured into the country from eastern and southern Europe.

This was in contrast to the earlier surge of immigrants from northern and western Europe in the late 19th century, lured by the hope of cheap land out west. These immigrants, coming from roots similar to those of earlier Americans, melded into the rural society reasonably well and quickly.

Times changed, and as the 19th century ended and the 20th century began, factories in need of cheap labor were beginning to sprout in the cities. That's where the later immigrants gravitated, clustering together in ethnic neighborhoods and retaining the language and customs of the old country.

Interestingly, different ethnic groups seem to be drawn to different kinds of work. They say that the Italians built the bridges, railroads, and sewers; Poles, Czechs, and Hungarians went into the mines and the steel plants; Greeks opened restaurants; and Russian Jews went into the clothing, chain store, and entertainment businesses.

While the earlier Jewish immigrants from Germany assimilated more easily into American culture, Jews from Eastern Europe and Russia tended to be Orthodox and very strict in following Judaic rules and rituals. It was also during this time that Jews became the focus of religious discrimination in the New World in place of the Roman Catholics. This would affect my father and mother and the rest of us for all our lives. Even to this day, I feel that it's an uphill battle to succeed in a land dominated by another culture.

My parents lives were drastically changed when World War I broke out in 1914. The war did not involve the United States until four years later, but the turmoil and restrictions made it impossible for my mother to come to America until 1922.

My father arrived in America ready to work as a tailor, and work he did, for $5 a week in a small backroom along with his brother, Charles, and six other tailors.

He moved in with Charles to save money, but he could see that at $5 a week it would be a long time before he could save enough money to send for Sarah.

In Russia, my mother and the children were surviving under tough conditions. There was no job she could do to earn a living because she lacked the training and women didn't work outside the home. She did have the training to be a survivor and that's what she did for herself and the three children.

Still, it had to be hard. Hard to make sure there was food on the table and wood for the fire in the winters. To get food, she and the children became gleaners. They trudged to distant fields in the cold and carefully picked through the harvested rows to find grains of wheat spilled by the farmers as they harvested.

How did my mother last ten years living on the razor's edge of existence? I am not sure, but I believe it was because of her dream and her determination. She had a dream that she would some day hear again from her husband in America and he would send for her. Because of the war and the revolution, it was years before a letter came from him, but she was kept alive by her dream.

And there was her determination. She refused to give up. She started each day by promising herself that she would make it through for herself and for her children.

My children and my colleagues say I have the same ability to have a dream and the determination to strive toward it. Certainly I know I have many of the same traits my mother had.

On November 2, 1920, Conservative Warren Harding swept into office by a landslide over Democrat James M. Cox. Six days later, the Russian civil war ended as the White Army evacuated the Crimea, bringing an uneasy peace to the Ukraine around Koretz.

Finally, in 1922, four years after World War I was over, my father had saved enough to send for mother and the children.

She told me that she was able to get a ride for herself and the children from Koretz to Warsaw in a wagon load of straw. It took three weeks because of the war-torn countryside, torn up roads, demolished bridges, and marauding bands of discharged hungry and homeless soldiers. When mother and the children left, they could take nothing except the clothes they had on their backs and some bread stuffed into their pockets.

As Louis had done ten years before, the four got on a ship as shabby as the cattle boat he had been on. The food was just as bad, but that didn't matter since all four of them were deathly seasick the whole trip and couldn't keep food down.

They followed the footsteps of my father through Ellis Island, only this time my father was there to greet them.

It was a pitiful sight in many ways.

My mother, the children, and all the other passengers, in their threadbare outfits, had filed down the gangplank with their tiny handfuls of belongings and followed the immigration officer across the landing dock to the Great Hall on Ellis Island.

Bureaucrats cross-examined them, and complex names were routinely Americanized on the spot. Rothenstein became Ross and Liedencasen became Linder, but Nirenberg remained Nirenberg.

When my mother finished her processing, she grasped another official piece of paper, this one covered with rubber stamps instead of the Imperial Czarist ribbons and red wax. Moments later she had a hugging, joyful reunion with the husband she had not seen in ten years.

Mother came to a new America, an America molded by new inventions and new social movements that would change the nation radically. America had emerged from 19th Century culture to become a more free and liberal society. These changes would be the basis of my business success and the fulfillment of my mother's ultimate dream.

The impact of the automobile was tremendous because it provided jobs, long distance mobility, and privacy for people away from home. Imagine my mother's reaction coming from rural Russia to a place where the roads were filled with cars!

Henry Ford was a key figure in the automobile revolution, because he learned how to turn out the Model T for the relatively inexpensive price of $208 while paying his workers the unheard-of wage of $5 a day. This made it possible for Ford workers to buy what they built. By 1925, Ford had sold an astonishing 15 million cars.

During that same decade, two policies of the Federal government affected millions of Americans in general and the Nirenberg family in particular: they were the Two New Prohibitions —one social and one political.

The social prohibition, imposed on the country by the conservatives, prohibited people from making, selling, or transporting alcoholic beverages. [It was okay to store or drink them.] This was called Prohibition or the Noble Experiment by some and foolishness by others. Whatever it was, it helped the Nirenberg family survive.

The revolt against Prohibition gave birth to the wealth of some of America's great families, like the Kennedys of Massachusetts, the state where my family lived. In a significant, but very minor way, Prohibition helped the Nirenberg family, too, by providing us a business with which to buy our farm in Millis.

The second or political prohibition was against unrestricted immigration and was aimed at people like my mother—Russian Jews from the Ukraine.

The political prohibition symbolized the fear the predominantly Anglo-Protestant class in America had about preserving their culture in the face of the onslaught of immigration by people from the Mediterranean and East European countries.

Equally disturbing to conservatives was the flood of new immigrants—mostly Roman Catholics and Jews—coming into the country since 1890 and bearing radical ideas.

Before World War I, anybody who wanted to immigrate to the United States could do so, with the exception of Asians, prostitutes, imbeciles, and the poor. Two unlikely forces joined to reverse that policy: the Anglo-Protestant rich and the blue collar labor unions. If the new law caused by this change in policy had been enacted a few months earlier, I would never have been born.

Labor unions saw unrestricted immigration as providing an endless stream of hungry, cheap labor, which made organizing unions impossible. Until there was a shortage of labor, the unions would never get into a strong bargaining position.

The rich management class and the intellectuals it supported feared immigrants from anywhere but northern Europe, from which the majority of them came. Mediterranean and Eastern European people were thought to be revolutionaries and nonconformist thinkers, thus, a menace to American society. One commentator warned that continuing unlimited immigration would produce a hybrid race of good-for-nothing mongrels.

Fortunately, my mother, brothers, and sister made the journey before the most restrictive of these laws, the Immigration Act of 1924, was signed into law. If they hadn't, they would have been murdered by the Communists or gassed by the Nazis for certain. I know, because that's what happened to the rest of the Jews who stayed in Koretz.

CHAPTER IV

Making It in America

ALTHOUGH MY MOTHER and father had been apart for ten years, it was clear that they were back together in a family context because my mother was soon pregnant with me.

She, father, and the children moved into the three-room, fourth-floor walk-up on Harrison Avenue, in a very poor section of Boston. And in December, 1923, the Nirenbergs had another Chanukah present in the house—one named after uncle Charlie, whose letter to Koretz 12 years before had triggered the saga that brought our family to Boston.

Now there were six of us stuffed into that little apartment with the train tracks outside the window and the street noises outside the door. Not only was it crowded, but it was tough on the family budget.

It was a time when people were moving away from the farm to the burgeoning cities to create new forms of society. The central form of individual transportation, the horse, was rapidly being replaced by the automobile. At the same time, American women were beginning to move out of the kitchen and nursery into the work force.

Certainly my mother was emerging out of the kitchen in our crowded apartment. It was noisy and crowded, but it was home and, if we were poor we didn't know it, because everyone else in the neighborhood was also poor.

A lot of people were making money in the stock market, and while my mother and I couldn't get into the stock market, we had something else going on the side. Obviously, I was too young to realize it, but when I was only half-a-year old, my mother and I went into business together.

Every day my father went to work in that little room with the other tailors to earn his now increased salary of $10 a week. Still, it was not enough when there were six to feed, clothe, and house.

So, my mother, following the central philosophy of successful business—find a need and fill it—found a need and filled it. Actually, she was doing a lot of filling. It was Prohibition, and she noticed there seemed to be an awful lot of thirsty people who always had money for something that would relieve their thirst and boost their spirits, so to speak. So mother started making booze in a small still in our apartment and filling half-pint bottles she bought at the drug store. Then she went out on the street and sold them.

It worked this way: 16 flat half-pint bottles fit perfectly under the mattress of my baby carriage. She would fill 16 bottles from the still in our apartment, carry them down four flights, arrange the bottles in the baby carriage, and cover them with the mattress and me.

Out on the street she was pleasant and maternal-looking to everyone, including the policeman on the beat who would stop and talk with her and inquire about my health. If the visit lasted too long, she would discreetly pinch me and I would start crying, while the policeman suddenly found he had to move along his beat.

The chances are that the policeman knew what was going on, because he knew about the speakeasy and the stores that regularly sold booze under the counter and did nothing about it. Times were tough, and people had to do what they had to do to survive. Being a bootlegger was nothing to brag about, but in later years I would find out that a number of family fortunes were made in that and other illegal ways. Besides, mother made good alcohol. No one every got sick or died from it as happened with some other moonshiners' products. It was a philosophy I would later apply to the products I made: always go for quality—people can tell and they will appreciate it.

My father didn't take particular notice of mother's bootlegging until he found out that she made more money than he did. Then, he wanted to quit tailoring, but I can imagine the conversation that followed that idea, "No, Louis, you must continue working in the tailor shop."

"Why? With what you are earning, Sarah, there is no need for me to work there in that crowded room."

"If you quit, people will wonder where we get our money and, soon they will find out. Then we will all be together in a crowded little room called jail."

Besides, father's continued associations at work produced a big change in our lives and, unintentionally, helped set me on the road to the business in which I would make a fortune. Aside from putting shoes on our feet and food in our stomach, mother's bootlegging business was going to get us out of Boston and away from Harrison Avenue, with its pushing crowds, noisy cars and trains. It was going to get us a farm in the country.

It happened because my father kept working at the tailor shop and got to talking with a co-worker who, like everyone else in those times, had a second job to help make ends meet. He was a real estate salesman, and he would change my life even though I never knew his name. Real estate transactions would become a big part of my career in later years, but this first one that affected me was quite significant.

I was about one year old when this other tailor cum real estate salesman sold my father on the idea of buying a farm in the town of Millis, about 20 miles outside of Boston. He convinced my father that one of the great advantages would be all the vegetables we could get free. He would never again have to worry about having something to eat.

The pitch was that my father would have a big garden with radishes and cucumbers and tomatoes and potatoes, so he would always have food on the table. If there was one thing that appealed to my father, it was to never again have to worry about having to earn money to feed his family. There had been too many nights of going to bed hungry in Koretz.

To my father, who knew nothing about farming, that

sounded wonderful. He didn't know anything about seeds and planting and cultivating and the rest, but it didn't matter.

To my mother, it was a good idea for many reasons. She understood about the farming part because of the ten years she struggled to stay alive in Koretz, when she had to know what farmers did. She liked the idea of getting her children out of the dirty, crowded city into the fresh air and sunshine of the country.

And there was something else—something buried in the psyche of every European peasant. It is probably passed along in the genes. It is the tantalizing dream of having a piece of land of your own. In land-scarce Europe, owning land had been the privilege of the rich and the aristocracy.

It meant that my father would have to commute to the city with another man who had a car and would be gone from home even more than he was already. But, the thought of having ten acres—TEN ACRES—of land, with a farm house and a chicken coop, was too much to resist. It was, incidentally, the money that mother had put aside from bootlegging that made the downpayment possible.

What a day it was when we moved! They had bought the property sight-unseen, but to my mother, it was unbelievable that she should have come to America barely two-and-a-half years before and now they owned ten acres of land in the country!

We had been living on the farm for four years or so when that bewildering day came about which I have already told you —the day of the red wagon and the fire.

In 1927, the whole country went crazy over Charles Lindbergh's solo flight across the Atlantic. Lucky Lindy's flight was an American triumph and something we marveled about even in Millis. Imagine crossing the Atlantic ocean in one day! Only five years before it had taken mother and the children a nauseated two weeks or more.

Times seemed prosperous under President Coolidge. America was caught up in the craze of marathon dance contests; sales of radios and phonographs skyrocketed; and everybody was getting into the stock market with only 10% down.

Three weeks before my birthday and the red wagon and house fire, the Republicans succeeded in putting a civil engineer from California, Herbert Hoover, into the White House, defeating Alfred E. Smith, the first Roman Catholic ever nominated by a major U.S. party.

Back in Millis, after the place had been rebuilt enough to live in, we moved out of the Maels' house across the road and picked up the pieces of our life in the house where so many people in my family would live.

Early most mornings, a car would come by our house and pick up my father for the 20-mile trip to the tailor shop where he still worked. The same car driven by a friend would drop him off late at night. In spite of his hard work and long hours, he was still getting paid less than it cost to support the six of us.

So there was also another car that came by occasionally—a mysterious car that pulled around to the back of the house after dark, stopped for a few minutes and drove back down our pebble driveway, making a kind of crunching noise in the night.

We weren't told of the details, but Prohibition was still on. Mother had retained her still and made enough booze to cover the monthly payment on the farm.

Booze was a blessing for us in a way and a curse in another way. Bootleg booze helped support the family. That was the blessing. However, my father began to use booze to boost his sense of worth in the face of hard times, and it soon took control of him. That was the curse. It would cause some terrible problems in the time to come.

My mother planted a garden where I helped as best as a small kid can, pulling weeds, watering, and the assorted other minor chores I could do. We also started taking in boarders and always looked for ways to cut expenses.

> *They were very poor, and they had a boarding house in Millis, Massachusetts, and Bubbe would go to the Kosher butcher and she would tell the butcher that she needed bones for the dog and she'd take the bones and she'd make some kind of stew for the family. Then, finally give it to the dog.*
>
> —My Daughter Pam

So, for those first six years, my life centered around my mother. One morning when I turned six, it was time for me to start school. I went out to stand on the road in front to catch the school bus, but it didn't come and I had to go. So, I ran into the house to the bathroom and came out just in time to see the yellow bus go whizzing by without me. Naturally, I began to cry. This brought my parents on the run. My father took me by the hand and we walked the mile to my new school.

There I was immediately nicknamed "Sunshine" by my teacher, Miss Ellen Horan and—at the same time—faced one of the biggest surprises of my young life.

CHAPTER V

Teen Tycoon

STARTING SCHOOL WAS a significant change in my life because I was leaving the cocoon of home and expanding into the real world. That first day that my father dropped me off at Miss Horan's one-room school with the first three grades all together, I got the biggest surprise of my life up until then: I couldn't talk with the other people there.

I discovered everybody else talked English and I talked Yiddish and, while I could write my own name, it was only in Hebrew!

Miss Horan was nice and understanding, though. I soon picked up English, and she began calling me "Sunshine," because she said I had a happy disposition and loved being at school.

At home there were always chores that had to be done. It was part of family life and everybody was expected to do their share. My mother would teach me how to do things and then praise me when I did them right. I never complained. Certain things were expected of me at home and I always did my job before I played. I still do my job before I take time to play tennis. That may be the most important lesson I learned from my mother while growing up.

As part of my growing up about this time, that summer I got

involved with a club of about a dozen boys—naturally, no girls allowed—that had a little club house. We decided we could have more fun if we had a little money in the kitty to buy things. Trouble was that the nickel a week we set for dues was beyond the means of some of the members. That's when I suggested we figure out something to sell with the profits going to the club.

It just so happened that I had a product in mind. I used the same approach my mother had used in going into the bootleg business: find a need and fill it. I figured that every club member had a mother, grandmother, aunt, or big sister who had an ironing board, so I suggested we sell each of them a waxed ironing board pad. We could buy them for 30 cents each and sell them for 50 cents, making 20 cents for the club. That worked real well except we ran out of customers quickly.

It was during the early years of the Depression and everybody had a headache, so I decided to serve another need by selling aspirin. I bought a bottle of 500 aspirins for 99 cents and sold them two for a nickel. I needed packages for the two aspirins, and mother suggested I buy the little glassine envelopes the druggist used. It was a wonderful idea—one of many I got from her over my years in business—but there was one catch.

The druggist wanted to know why this seven-year old wanted to buy 250 envelopes. When he found out, he said he wouldn't sell them to me. He said I was competing with him. He only made a few cents profit on selling 500 aspirins for 99 cents, whereas I would make $6.51 profit less the cost of the envelopes!

Obviously he hadn't figured out that he could do the same thing. It was simply a matter of packaging and marketing a product people wanted in a form they wanted. This didn't take a rocket scientist to figure out, but he was going to thwart me because I figured it out and he didn't. Ironically, this was the first, but not the last, time this would happen to me in my business career.

I was saved in this instance by our family doctor, who happened to be in the store at the time. When he learned what was going on, he laughed and said admiringly that I was going to be some businessman when I grew up. Afraid of appearing mean-spirited, the druggist gave in and sold me the envelopes for 25 cents.

As I walked back to the club house to meet with my compatriot capitalists and tell them of our new project, I calculated in my head that 99 cents for the aspirin plus 25 cents for the envelopes totaled $1.24, which meant a net profit for the club of $6.26. Sounded great, but I was about to learn an important business lesson: you have to figure in the possibility of having surplus inventory.

Repackaging the aspirins turned out to be a lot more work than everybody was anxious to do, and after going all over Millis peddling our wonderful product, we came back with a lot unsold. So we divided up the aspirin that were left and that was part of our pay.

Even so, we made some profit for the club. More importantly for me, I had discovered something about myself at age seven that a lot of people don't discover until they're in their twenties or thirties. Namely, I subconsciously found out what I wanted to be even before I grew up. I wanted to be a businessman. I was excited, fascinated and strangely fulfilled by the simple process of thinking up a product people would want and merchandising it for a profit. What a way to make a living and to have a life.

In my new-found calling for which I had such enthusiasm, I talked my fellow club members into going for something big. The aspirin deal was penny ante stuff, I told them. We should go for dollars with our next project.

Here was the plan: I had heard that they were paying $3 apiece for skunk pelts, and there were a lot of skunks in the woods on the edge of Millis. The connection was obvious, but this time I wanted the whole gang to vote on investing our money in skunk traps. We voted and they all went for it. We bought six traps, set them out in the woods, baited them with chicken bones, and agreed to take turns checking them.

Seymour and I had the first shift. When we found a live skunk trapped in our first trap, we were so excited that we took it out and headed for my house to show off our prize. My mother was not impressed because the skunk had drenched us in its smelly spray: we stunk from skunk and my mother put an end to the project immediately.

It took two weeks for Seymour and me to smell normal again. During that time, the club met and decided we had made a business miscalculation and declared a dividend of the six traps.

We did several other money-making projects that summer before we split up the kitty and returned to school that fall.

I guess that was the summer when the get-into-business-for-yourself bug bit me. By trial and error, I had found the formula for running a business and making some money as a result. For the lessons I learned pretty much apply to any business.

I am not sure what it was inside of me that pushed me to take the lead in the kind of business projects we did in our little boys' club and during the rest of my life. Someone once said I reminded them of a saying by Oakland football coach and TV sports commentator, John Madden,

> "There are three kinds of people. People who make things happen. People who watch things happen. And, people who don't know what's happening."

I guess I am the first kind. While I had learned how to make money in my little world that summer, things were pretty bad elsewhere in the country.

In the Twenties, the country was enjoying what seemed to be an endless prosperity, with most people caught up in the grip of the stock market game. They could buy stocks for 10% down, and as long as the stock prices kept going up, they were making money without having to ante up any more. It seemed like a magical golden spinning wheel.

Henry Ford became the wonderman of industry by turning out a new car every 17 seconds, until there were 26 million cars on the roads of America. The Republican government led by Calvin Coolidge, who proclaimed that the business of America was business, had helped business burst with production and prosperity, with corporate profits rising 62% from 1923 to 1929.

This was not the philosophy of other industrialists, however. Worker's pay from 1923 to 1929 only rose by 11 percent, and the mass of people stopped buying anything but essentials. Soon farm income dropped sharply, inventories rose, and people started getting laid off, which cut consumption even more.

We were touched by the drop in farm income. We had two cows, and I was milking them twice a day, which was my early association with a product that would become central to my life thereafter. Unfortunately, there wasn't much of a market for milk. In fact, the price of milk had gone so low that farmers in some dairy states were besieging their state capitals and dumping thousands of gallons into the sewers in protest, with the press watching.

Still, on the facade it looked as though America was doing great. But at 11 o'clock on the morning of Thursday, October 24, 1929, America began to unravel. What had started as a routine day on the stock market suddenly turned into a frenzy of piranha fish, as someone noticed a mountain of sell orders unmatched by buy orders and panicked. In minutes, the telegraph and telephone lines were overloaded and the ticker tape fell further and further behind, leaving investors deaf, dumb, blind, and hysterical. Screaming, jumping traders saturated the trading floor, and stock prices plummeted as brokers desperately tried to telephone investors to demand more money to cover the losses.

A group of bankers rushed in several hours later and began buying stocks to stabilize the market and calm the unnerved traders. The next day things seemed to return to normal, and President Hoover pronounced that the fundamental business of America was sound and solid. Nine days later, the worst bank failure in American history took place when the Bank of the United States went under.

The market began dropping, dropping, dropping again on Monday, Tuesday, and on into November. On Black Tuesday, November 29th, when the entire market collapsed, fortunes and near-fortunes were ruined, and people were afraid to go outside in the Financial District for fear of being hit by a falling body.

Comedian Eddie Cantor, who lost $2 million in the Crash, said New York hotel clerks now asked people renting a room, "For sleeping or for jumping?"

There had been warnings to which no one listened, of course. Economist Roger Babson and Alexander Noyes, financial editor of the *New York Times*, warned their readers of a coming financial crisis, but everyone was too busy making a fortune to hear them.

I was too young to understand it all and, besides, our family didn't have a fortune to lose. We were already poor, except for the garden, two cows, and some chickens.

We had our own problems being poor. By 1932, Prohibition had been repealed and mother's bootlegging business died. And, as I said, selling milk was a lost cause. I was nine, my brother Barney was 25, my sister Ann was 23, my brother Morris was 20 and the baby, Joe, was five. My father had become an alcoholic. He withdrew into himself and became a very embittered human being. He had had a great deal of luck during his lifetime, but all of it was bad. The older kids had their own lives, and Joe was too young. So it came down to Mother and me struggling to make ends meet.

School was out and I tried to find a job, but dozens of grown men would compete against me for what, in better times, was a kid's job. While I was home trying to figure out what to do, I realized that, while we might not be able to sell our milk as readily as we wanted, there seemed to be a good market for eggs. I guess it was a low-cost, healthy food that people could afford in this time of the Great Depression.

We were on a well-traveled road from Boston, and I set up a stand, hand-lettered a sign out of a cut-up cardboard box and red Crayola—"EGGS 39¢ A DOZEN"—and was in business. On the first day, a man stopped and asked if my eggs were fresh—freshness has always been a big deal with food and with eggs in particular. On the spur of the moment, I answered, "Fresh from the chicken's nest." He bought the only dozen eggs I sold all day.

The next day I changed the sign, "PICK YOUR OWN FRESH EGGS FROM THE CHICKEN'S NEST." We were sold out by noon.

> *"Charlie is sensitive to the importance of images: I think consumers have to believe they're buying a good product. You can have the best product in the world, but if you don't TELL 'em it's a great product, if you don't LOOK like a great product, they'll never BELIEVE it's a great product.'"*

—Patricia Wright writing in MASSACHUSETTS:
The Magazine For Alumni and Friends of the University of Massachusetts, Winter of 1992—
60 years *after* Charlie was in the egg business in front of his farmhouse in Millis.

I had learned another great business lesson and, without even knowing the business jargon, I had taught myself the difference between selling and merchandizing. Selling is just trading a product for money. Merchandizing is promoting, establishing a need, and distributing a product.

So I decided I could merchandize eggs, but I didn't have enough inventory to handle the customers. That's when I went across the road to my chicken farmer neighbors and asked if they had any eggs they would like to sell me wholesale. They did, and I took their several dozen and put them under the hens in our chicken coop. We were sold out again by midafternoon.

Naturally, I figured I was on to something, and I expanded my route to five other farms. I bought up all the eggs they could spare and was selling 30 dozen eggs a week from my 12 chickens while clearing $3 to $5 a week. That was close to what grown men were making in those days.

As the summer of 1933 approached, I decided I really needed more chickens of my own because, if I didn't have to buy eggs from other farmers, I would make a lot more money. Mother explained to me about roosters and hens, and I bought a rooster and let the eggs stay under the hens until a horde of fluffy, peeping baby chicks was swarming all over the place.

Whenever the egg business tapered off, I would sell the hens to a butcher shop and make money that way. The one thing that was too tough for me was to kill and dress my own chickens. My deal with the butcher was that he took them live, and I never had to deal with the messy end of the business.

I could keep the baby broilers until they were 12 weeks old, or I could sell them when they weighed a little less at eight weeks. I decided to sell them when they were eight weeks old because I calculated that the cost of chicken feed for those extra four weeks wasn't chicken feed. It cost more to feed the chickens for four weeks than I got in return for the extra weight they gained.

To me, at age 12, this was fairly simple to figure out. Years later, I would find out to my amazement that people went to graduate school to earn a Masters in Business Administration [MBA] to learn how to do this. To me, it is common sense business. To an MBA it is cost-benefit analysis.

By the time I was 12, we had 5,000 chickens and two cows. It was good for the family, but I don't think it was good for my father's self-image.

One night I sat down at our kitchen table and explained to him what I was doing. He hadn't been that interested before—partially because he would be too drunk or too tired most nights. Anyhow, I told him what I was doing in the chicken and egg business. He was amazed and, I think, depressed to find out I was contributing more money to the family than he was.

It may have been a mistake to tell him.

CHAPTER VI

A Shift of Careers at 14

THERE WAS SOMETHING strange about those youthful years, but I didn't realize it at the time.

I was always MAKING money in some way in spite of the hard times, but I never seemed to HAVE any money. The supreme irony was that I, a man who would later make a fortune selling ice cream, couldn't afford to buy an ice cream cone from Nick the Greek when he came around peddling his delicious, cold treats. Nick took pity on me and occasionally gave me an empty sugar cone to munch on while the other kids were licking their ice creams. I never forgot both his kindness and his sales savvy and, a few years later, he was working for me.

NICK'S SALES SAAVY

Nick sold more ice cream than his competing peddlers because he had special sense. He looked foreign and some of the kids thought he was not too bright so they would short change him. A smart aleck would slip him four pennies for an ice cream instead of the regular five pennies.

Nick would simply pocket the money without looking at it or counting. That was his sales trick.

He knew that some kids would short change him, but it didn't make any difference, Nick was still making a profit. But, by letting the smart aleck kids get away with it, Nick was getting customers other peddlers weren't getting. In essence, he was willing to sell at an unintended discount in exchange for doing a volume business.

So, Nick was smart enough to pretend to be dumb.

What I made, of course, went to my mother because my family needed that money to survive. It never bothered me because it was expected of me, and I have always tried to do what was expected of me. I never spent any money until I had asked my mother if it would be all right.

This is where I part with today's parents. Today's kids are used to going to mom or dad when they want something, and they get it. I don't blame the kids, but I wonder about the wisdom of giving a child everything he asks for—no, that's not right. I don't wonder about that. I know it is not good for either the kid or the parent.

That's why I drew the line with my kids and the business. There was always a job for any of my kids working in my company, but that didn't mean there was an executive position or featherbed for any of them. They could get in the door because they were my kids, but what they became after they got in the door was up to them to earn.

That attitude is part of the way I was raised. As old-fashioned as it sounds, we did what our parents told us to do, and we don't seem to be the worse off for it. My mother's word was law in our family. For example, I loved to play baseball and football in pick-up games, but I couldn't do it on the school team. When I said I wanted to go out for the school team, my mother told me in Yiddish, "You can break a leg playing football. I don't want you to do it, Charlie." And that was that. Most kids in those days did what their parents told them to do. My, how times have changed!

Or have they? I learned a lot of good things from my mother, and I guess my respect for her gave her the ability to steer me in the right direction. Still, kids have always rebelled against the authority of their parents. Even though I didn't feel that way about my mother, I did rebel against my father, and my children, in their time, would rebel against me.

A friend once quoted an old man's assessment of teenagers to me. The old man said, "Children today have no respect for their elders. They don't listen, they don't obey. They just run wild without discipline." That old man was right. He was Socrates, who lived in Ancient Greece 2500 years ago.

An example of both the tragedy of my father and his alcoholism focused on the rebellion of one of the kids in my own family: my brother Morris, whom I idolized. Born in Koretz a year before my father left for America, he and my other older brother, Barney, and my sister, Ann, endured those terrible ten years together.

Morris influenced my life immensely, and I still remember his rebellion against my father. Back when I was only six and Morris was 17, Mother and Father got into a terrible argument. I suspect that my father had been drinking and my mother was angry about it. They were shouting at each other, and most of us were shrinking from their rage, when my father raised his hand and moved to hit my mother.

In an instant, Morris was between them and punched my father before he could strike our mother. It was a courageous thing for him to do, but my father banished him from the house for it.

Now we had a curious situation that sometimes happens in families. My mother, always the strong one in the marriage and the family, was saved from being assaulted by my father, who rarely earned the stature from us that a father should have in a family. At that moment, however, he invoked his authority as head of the family—probably the only time I can remember him doing that. It would be some time before I understood it, but my mother immediately became the Old World wife and deferred to him as the titular head of the house. Morris had to leave! It was confusing to a six-year-old.

Morris found a room a half-mile away, and each night before my father got home from work, Mother would walk that half-mile to bring a hot meal to Morris. Mother always walked everywhere because it was quite European for a woman to walk; besides which we didn't have a car.

Mother also kept Morris supplied with food for breakfast

and sandwiches and kept it secret from her husband. If he had known, there would have been another fight, because he had been raised to believe that the man was king in his home and no one should dare challenge him. Mother, always the maverick, listened to him and then found a way to do things the way they should be done.

At home, families stared at a Philco radio shaped like a cathedral arch and let their imaginations create the theater of the mind. "Dick Tracy"; "The Shadow"; "Jack Armstrong The All American Boy"; "Jack Benny"; "Fibber McGee and Molly"; and "Amos and Andy" were some of the hits of the time.

Herbert Hoover, a well-meaning wealthy engineer, never understood what happened on his watch at the White House. He failed to do what the government could have done to prevent the economic disaster that befell America in 1929 and the 1930s.

Millions were out of work and demanding help, but Hoover did nothing because he thought it was not the job of the government. When thousands of veterans marched on Washington, D.C., demanding bonuses that had been promised them, Hoover ordered the army to drive them out. The officer in charge of driving out these homeless veterans was a colonel by the name of Dwight David Eisenhower who, in turn, was under the orders of General Douglas MacArthur. Years later, General Dwight David Eisenhower would be my Commander-in-Chief.

In New York City there were 17,000 evictions a month. Former bankers and stock brokers were selling apples in suits and ties on street corners, and the Democrats chose a spoiled rich man's son as their 1932 nominee for president, Franklin D. Roosevelt [FDR]. Just like the last Democrat to be elected president, Woodrow Wilson, Roosevelt wore pince-nez glasses. Accepting the nomination, Roosevelt told the delirious Democratic convention, "I pledge you, I pledge myself, to a New Deal for the American people."

At the same time, turmoil was erupting around the globe. The Chinese Communists made their epic Long March; Francisco Franco fomented the Spanish Civil War; and Hitler and his National Socialist German Worker's Party seized control of

Germany, vowing a reborn nation and the eradication of Jews, gays and Communists.

Jumping ahead again to when I was 14 and getting out of the chicken and egg business, Morris had gone on with his life, married, and gotten into the ice cream business.

He had an ice cream truck just like Nick the Greek's and drove around neighborhoods selling ice cream—mostly to parents who bought it for their kids.

With ice cream it was the same thing as it was with the movies and radio that grownups used for a little respite from the tension of the times. Ice cream was a relatively inexpensive happiness that parents could give their children, at a time when there wasn't much else they could afford.

Morris would let me ride around with him on the truck, and I loved it. And selling ice cream even in the Depression looked as easy to me as selling eggs and chickens.

"Morris, how about me getting a job with you?"

He laughed and asked,

"What can you do for me?"

The question stumped me and I couldn't come up with an answer right away. But Morris, always looking out for his kid brother, had one:

"What if we get you a peddler's box with some dry ice and load it with ice cream bars and ice cream sandwiches, and I take you around to some of the factories in this area?

"You can go in and sell some ice cream. After I work the neighborhoods, I'll come back and pick you up a couple hours later. Then we can find out if you're a salesman."

I didn't need to find out if I was a salesman. I already knew that, but here I was making a career change and I was only 14 years old. That's how I spent the summer of 1938, right in the heart of the Depression, selling ice cream. I am still selling ice cream over 50 years later, but what a difference!

CHAPTER VII

Dry Ice Determination

THERE WERE TWO things I learned that summer, and both were important to my financial success.

The first thing I found out was that I still had some things to learn before I became as good a salesman as I already thought I was. I entered the big concrete sewer pipe factory on that hot June afternoon with my dry ice peddler's box slung over my shoulder. It contained four dozen chocolate-covered ice cream bars and four dozen ice cream sandwiches.

The concrete sewer pipes were constructed outside and it was hot. This battalion of big, rough-looking men milling around and filling the place with curse words was something I didn't completely understand. As I looked around, uncertain of my next move, one of them yelled at me, "What you got in the box, kid?"

Smiling my most engaging smile, "Nice, cold ice cream bars and sandwiches. Only five cents each."

"Hey, kid, speak up. I can hardly hear you. Tell everyone what you got in a voice so they can hear you."

"ICE CREAM, ICE CREAM HERE—ONLY 5 CENTS EACH!"

"That's better, kid. Gimme one."

I made my first ice cream sale—the first of millions more I

would make in the next half century—and I learned something new. I got my first lesson in how to sell ice cream: sing it out; let people know what you're selling; advertise to your market. You can't sell anything if nobody knows you have it for sale. It's a lesson I never forgot.

Of course, the more general lesson about life coming from this is that you must keep learning all the time. There is always something more you can learn. That first day in the sewer pipe factory, I learned an important selling lesson that would help me the rest of my life.

Here 54 years later I am writing a book and I am getting new perceptions of me as I write—new things about me, new things about my own family, and new things about my life.

"ICE CREAM, ICE CREAM HERE—ONLY 5 CENTS EACH!"

These big burly guys turned around and came crowding over to me, pushing nickels at me with that Ice Cream Look. I soon learned that there was this Ice Cream Look of anticipated pleasure that never came when people were buying laundry soap or newspapers or cucumbers. The Chinese emperor for whom the mixture of milk, rice and ice was invented as the first ice cream probably had the same look of anticipation of the pleasure of enjoying ice cream.

"What the fuckin' hell do you think you're doing?"

I wasn't exactly sure of the graphic meaning of the question coming from that charging bull disguised as Mr. Boss Man, but it was very clear to me that he was angry.

"This ain't no Goddamn ice cream social, kid, we got work to do here. Now get your fuckin' ass out of here and don't come back."

I put my tail between my legs and slunk out of the project, having sold a dozen ice creams. My brother found me sitting on the curb an hour later with my head hanging down to my shoe tops.

"What happened?"

I told him, but I didn't get what I thought I sorely needed at that moment: sympathy.

"Doesn't look to me like you have the guts to sell ice cream."

That did it. All the way home I was mad. I was mad at Morris. I was mad at Mr. Boss Man. I was mad at everyone except the right person. Then I got mad at me. That's who my mad should have been concentrated on in the first place.

"Morris, I'm going back there and show that guy I'm not afraid of him."

"Good. Think it out. Plan how you're going to do it. Then tomorrow we'll see if you know how to sell ice cream."

Another lesson learned. Ten minutes before, I thought I needed sympathy. My brother taught me I needed determination. I had never had my determination tested before, but now it was on the line and I was learning the most important lesson of success that life has to offer.

Determination—determination is the critical ingredient to success no matter what your goal is. Determination was what got my mother out of Koretz with her three children. Determination is the essence of most great achievements, whether it be Thomas Edison testing hundreds of different filaments before he perfected the light bulb or the American space program suffering failures before it succeeded in putting men on the moon.

> *Nothing in the world can take the place of determination. Talent will not; nothing is more common than unsuccessful men with talent; unrewarded genius is almost a proverb. Education will not; the world is full of educated derelicts. Persistence and determination alone are omnipotent. The slogan, "Press On" has solved and always will solve the problems of the human race.*
>
> —Calvin Coolidge

The next day I charged into the same construction site, but I was a different Charlie Nirenberg. I sold the same group of hot and eager workers two dozen ice creams before Mr. Boss Man started yelling and I started running.

Here again, it was different. This time I didn't run out of the project. I ran to the other side of the place and sold another two dozen ice creams to another crew. Quickly, it got to be a game, and the men were on my side. They wanted their ice cream. They had the Ice Cream Look on their faces.

They distracted Mr. Boss Man when they saw me coming and warned me when he spotted me again and started yelling once more. I don't think Mr. Boss Man's heart was really in it —chasing a little kid who was just trying to sell a few ice creams that his workers wanted anyhow. In the end, he begrudgingly let me slip in and out for a few minutes every day and I always sold out. Determination had won out once more!

Some years later I would hear the story of Harry Jamieson, a hardware salesman in the Northwest who had a reputation of being the most persistent, most determined salesman in the history of American business. He once called on a prospect 125 times in one year before he sold the man an order of hardware. When asked how many calls he would make on a prospect before giving up, Jamieson said, "It depends on which one of us dies first."

The workers in that sewer pipe factory were probably making ten or twelve dollars a week working a ten-hour day, and I was making that much working a couple of hours a day. Another lesson learned. I could use my head and earn a lot more than I would ever earn through physical labor.

Toward the end of this, my first summer in the ice cream business, I did get involved in something physical. It was the first dramatic confrontation I had with bigotry.

Oh, there had been earlier times when religious slurs were made against me and my family, but most of us learned to let them go even though I cannot say that it was always easy.

In fact, let me say it now: it was an uphill fight growing up a Jew in a Christian world, but I tried not to pay too much attention to it. As it is today, the bigots are not very many in number. They just have bigger mouths and more devious ways. Around this time, for example, there was the Massachusetts state legislator who tried to get a law passed requiring all comedians to use their "right" name so as to reveal the Jewish origins of entertainers such as Jack Benny, George Burns, and Eddie Cantor. We tried to ignore this kind of childish ignorance.

Besides, I don't really consider myself in terms of being a Jew. I am an American who just doesn't happen to belong to the majority faith. I respect the beliefs of my fellow Americans who are Christians or Moslems or Buddhists or whatever and only ask that they show me the same courtesy and respect in return. I think intelligent people of any religion or creed in America feel the same way.

However, that reasoned and philosophical approach was of no help with Mike Cassidy who, as you might guess, was an Irish Catholic. Somehow and for some reason that I don't remember today, Mike got off some choice expletives about me and my family and succeeded in triggering my hot button. All of a sudden, we two teenage boys with adrenaline racing were facing off in a fight.

I had never been in a real fist fight before, and I figured the chances of me getting my tail whipped were awfully good. I was not the physical type. Mike was. He was bigger and heavier, and I assumed he was a lot more experienced at fighting, because he had a reputation for going around looking for a fight with just about anybody and everybody. Physical aggressiveness and fighting were second nature to him. They weren't to me.

As we stood defying each other and circling slowly like two strange dogs when they first meet, I was scared. I knew I was in big trouble. This guy was going to beat the hell out of me and I knew it.

Still, there was one thing I was determined I was going to do and that was to get in at least one good punch before he beat me up. He was going to hurt me, I knew, but I wasn't going down without hurting him back.

With our fists up and my head down as I had seen the professional boxers do in movies, we each began probing our opponent. He moved in with his tongue hanging out of the corner of his mouth the way Michael Jordan's does when he drives in for a setup in basketball.

In a flash I saw an opening and let loose with an uppercut that I knew would be the only punch I would get in before the lights went out and darn near cut his tongue off. I hadn't planned it. It just happened that way.

Blood gushed over the front of his shirt, his hands went to his mouth in startled pain, and the strangest look of surprise flashed across his face as fear filled his eyes. I think I had an equally surprised look on my face, but I don't know for sure. I do know for sure that I was as surprised as Mike was. The fight was over before it really began.

I suppose at this point I should say that Mike and I became best friends after that, but we didn't. Let's just say that we understood each other and remained acquaintances who didn't bother each other any more.

By the end of that summer, I had earned over $100. This time, my mother refused to take the money for herself or the family. She told me to put it in the bank for my college education. I had had a savings account ever since I was five, when I got a silver dollar for that fateful birthday of the red wagon and house fire.

CHAPTER VIII

Ice Cream Peddler

As the 1930s ended, the United States was beginning to pull out of the Depression, and I was in the ice cream business and in high school.

There were still 10 million workers out of jobs, and America was trying to focus on itself and on getting well economically. Then World War II began on the morning of September 1, 1939, when I was just short of turning 16. The Nazi Blitzkrieg jabbed across the Polish border, and soon after, England and France declared war against Germany.

But at the time the war in Europe didn't mean all that much to me. More important at that moment, I had graduated from a bicycle to an ice cream truck. At this point in my life, ice cream had become my life. School was easy because I enjoyed it and waltzed through most of my classes, but what I really had fun doing was selling—selling ice cream.

Selling ice cream affected my schooling to some extent, because the ice cream season was April 1 to August 31. For the last six weeks of the spring semester, my grades would drop to B's. The rest of the time, from September 1 to March 31, I earned mostly A's.

Let's face it, I was a hooked peddler. Amazingly, it was an easy way to make really good money during what were hard times for many other people. My brother, Morris, taught me a lot about the business, and I knew that ice cream would be important to building my future.

Morris and I worked together in the ice cream business. He would pack my ice cream truck and leave it parked in the back of my school. When I got out at two in the afternoon, I would pick up the truck and start driving around my neighborhood route.

We did well, as I said, even though times were hard for many people. I think it may have been for the same reason I was selling ice cream in the sewer pipe factory. A nickel ice cream was an inexpensive luxury or treat for the kids that people could afford. It was tasty and made life a little more bearable when everything else in people's worlds was gray.

I was on my ice cream route until 11 o'clock every night. That meant, from the beginning of ice cream season at the start of April until fall, I didn't get a whole lot of sleep. I tried to do my homework before I left school. When I got home I did some more, but mostly I would eat and talk with my dying father around the kitchen table.

Most of the truck peddlers just went out to the same neighborhoods and did the same routes day after day. They never seemed to care about doing much more than making enough money to get by. When they reached their quota for the day, they would wheel the truck around gratefully and head for home.

That wasn't me. I figured out that people were up late during the summer, and I did some of my best business after nine o'clock. Even so, six to nine was regularly the best selling time, with two to six the worst.

I thought about why two to six was the worst time. Where were the best customers then? The same place they were when I was peddling out of a dry ice box—at work. Here was another simple, but important lesson of sales learned: go where your customers are. You can't sell merchandise where the customers aren't.

So I left school in my truck and immediately headed for a nearby factory that had a 15-minute break at 2:30 and was always good for 20 to 30 fast sales. I expanded on this in 1940 and later because defense work was picking up sharply.

I paid attention to my customers even in those simple days, because it dawned on me that it was important to know my customers. Know what my customers liked and disliked. That hasn't changed in the way I do business to this very day. People like to do business with people who like them and understand their needs. No miraculous secret, but a truth that surprisingly few businessmen seem to grasp.

The change in my customers was that, for the first time since I was born, people had some spare money to spend without feeling guilty about it. The wife and kids were finally getting some of the things they wanted and needed, and factory workers were buying more ice cream. And parents were not only buying ice cream off my truck for their kids, they were buying some ice cream for themselves, too.

The factories were staying open later and working two shifts. I had one factory where I could walk through at ten o'clock and sell $20 to $30 worth in less than an hour.

In all honesty, this easy money was probably spoiling me. Since I had been a junior in high school, I had owned my own truck and an ice cream business. Still, most of my money went to my father's medical bills.

The relationship between me and my father was troubling. It was something that was not clear-cut or easily understood. Reams of psychology books have been written on the relationship between fathers and sons. I haven't read any of them—probably because it would be too painful.

I have heard it said that the life of a father is divided into two parts with his son. In the first part, he tries to get his son to obey him. In the second part, he tries to get his son to forgive him.

My father was a man who seemed to be dogged by bad luck. He never became the man that he hoped he would be. The luckiest things that happened to him came from my mother. He was lucky to have gotten her as a wife, although I suspect that she picked him rather than the other way around. He was lucky to have come to America, but was pushed into that by his wife. He was lucky to have a decent and loving home where his wife showed him the kind of respect that he longed for in the outside world.

Historically, the status of most men in their families relates to their success as a provider. My father was denied that dignity.

He loved being a master tailor, but it robbed him of the ability to make the kind of money needed to buy him the self-respect he yearned for in his life. During much of his life in America, his wife made as much money or more than he did. And when I said earlier that it was probably a mistake when I revealed to him that I made more money selling chickens and eggs than he did as a professional tailor, I was right. I was a teenager and I was earning more money than my father!

The contemplation of death has the power of focusing the mind wonderfully. What I do remember is that death focused my relationship with my father in an ironic way. His impending death brought us together and resolved some of our conflicts better than ever before. In that bizarre way, his dying last years were the most pleasant I remember with him.

My father was diagnosed with cancer and had to stop working. He came to terms with himself and his life and learned to live with bad luck. At the end, I believe he was no longer the bitter man that he had been for years. His dreams had not come true in America, but his son was living some of those dreams.

He would be waiting up for me every night when I came home from selling ice cream out of my bicycle cart and, later, my truck. We would sit at the kitchen table of that farmhouse in Millis and count the money I had made that day. We always ended the day together with me having a little supper and listening to him tell me how proud he was of me.

Looking back on those nights we shared together as father and son, man to man, I find it hard to write these words without feelings welling up inside of me. Those were precious moments for me, with a very special meaning even to this day that no one else can ever completely understand.

I cleared $100 a week, which was big money to him, and I was just a kid in high school. Come to think of it, that was big money to just about anyone in those days. But I worked hard to get it.

Much of the money I saved for college went instead to my

father's medical bills during my last two years in high school. He lay in the hospital for a time, but insisted on coming home as he sensed death coming closer. For him, the best medicine was waiting up for me and talking.

I began to look forward to it, too. We were able to say and be things to each other late at night in the kitchen that we had never been able to in all the years leading up to that time. He never told me, because men didn't say such things in those days, but I knew that he really loved me as I did him. We were never so close as we were that last year.

When the end was near, he called me into his bedroom one night and told me two things.

"I am going to give you this ring, son. I want you to have it, and when you have a son, I want you to pass it on to him before you die.

The ring he gave me had two holes in it where there had once been a diamond and a ruby. He had taken the diamond out and sold it so my sister could have a wedding. I don't know what happened to the ruby, but it, too, was gone. There were two Hebrew letters on the right that meant "To Life."

The ring had little monetary value, but it meant a lot to me because it was a symbol. It was all my father had to leave to his son after a lifetime of toil. It left me with mixed feelings.

He told me to give it to my son and I kept it for the memory of my father and to pass it on to my son, Larry. Unfortunately, my home was burglarized six weeks before my son's bar mitzvah and the ring was stolen so I couldn't carry out that wish of my father's.

I wanted to keep the ring because it was a memory of him and, whatever I felt about him during his lifetime, he still was my father. Still, I often thought of what a great relay race my business life could have been if he had had a business and passed the baton to me—but he really did leave me more: a healthy body and a good brain.

"Also, I want you to go down in the basement and you will find a fruit jar buried beneath my workbench. In it you will find $800—enough money for my funeral. I don't want anyone taking up a collection when I die.

"I will die with dignity because you have been a good son

and shared your good fortune with Mama and me. I won't ask you to take good care of Mama when I am gone because I already know you will."

Then he sighed and died before my eyes.

CHAPTER IX

New Lessons of Life

THERE ARE TIMES when I cannot control or suppress my emotions, and I found that out dramatically in 1941, my final year in high school.

Somehow, someday it came to me that little girls looked awfully nice and smelled awfully nice, and, before I knew it, I had fallen in love with Mimi Winiker. She was a year behind me in school, so I guess I was partial to younger women.

It won't come as a surprise to many people, but to me at the time, first love was a strange feeling. We called it puppy love with good reason. I was happy and excited as a puppy whenever I thought about her, and Mimi was on my mind night and day.

I was what we called a B.M.O.C. [Big Man On Campus] in those days and was confident that most of the girls in school noticed me, especially Mimi. After all, I was president of the Senior Class, Vice President of the Student Council, and editor of the school newspaper. Of course, she and I became steadies and everybody in Millis knew we were an item.

Then things mostly beyond my control began changing my life. First I graduated, leaving Mimi behind to finish high school while I worked to go to college. Then, the Sunday just six days before my 18th birthday, at 12:55 in the afternoon

Millis time, 200 single-engined airplanes swept low across the Hawaiian island of Oahu. Flight Commander Itaya broke radio silence to his pilots and shouted exuberantly the Japanese command to attack, "Tora! Tora! Tora!"

Twenty-five minutes later, the Japanese planes returned to their aircraft carriers and a second wave pounded Hickum Airfield and the Pearl Harbor Naval Base. By 2:45 Millis time, most of the U.S. fleet in the harbor was sunk or badly damaged.

The next day the President gave his "date that shall live in infamy" speech, and my life was changed in a way I hadn't counted on just twenty-four hours earlier. I thought college was out and the Army was in, but I ended up doing both.

I didn't have the money to start college when I graduated in 1941, so I took a job and learned another lesson about life in the little town of Millis.

I needed to earn some more money to make up what had been spent on my father's medical bills, so I started work in the Herman Shoe Factory. It was considered "the" factory in Millis. I mean, if you had to work in a factory, Herman was the one. Still, there was one thing I found out immediately that I didn't like about "the" factory in Millis.

In my department there were six women and two guys, Abie Winer and me. The women packed shoes into boxes for two cents a pair, and Abie's and my job was to give them empty boxes and take away full boxes. These women swore like troopers and used four-letter words that disgusted me. To me, women were so pure I didn't think they could swear.

The women worked fast because it was piece work, and they rarely quit, even to go to the bathroom. They packed shoes in the boxes five high, and then I took the five boxes and nestled them in a cardboard shipping crater. It was hectic, and everybody was moving as fast as they could. As they say, all you could see was asses and elbows.

Later, I would see the "I Love Lucy" comedy sequence where Lucy and Ethel were packing chocolates in a chocolate factory and I laughed and laughed. To other people, it was a comedy skit. To me it was my life at the Herman Shoe Company.

I made $14 for a five-and-a-half day week and would probably never make enough to pay for college. I had been there six weeks when I went in to see my boss.

"Mr. Flannigan, I'm going to give you my notice."
"Why, what's the matter, Charles? Can I give you a raise?"
"Mr. Flannigan, if you were to give me $2 more, I would still be only making $16 a week. Or, if you were to give me a $4 raise, I would only be making $18 a week. I don't think I'll ever become a millionaire doing this job!"
"You're serious, aren't you, Charles?"
"Yes, sir, Mr. Flannigan. I am very serious, but I want you to know that I'll stay on the job until you find my replacement."

The following week, Mr. Flannigan told me he had someone coming in on Monday, so I thought I was through. But the replacement failed to show up on Monday and he called me and asked if I would come back. He had been a very nice man, so I did. He was a gentlemen, so I decided I should be a gentleman. And he had taught me a lesson that I would carry the rest of my life.

Whenever he headed for the packing room, the word of his coming somehow proceeded him and anyone who was sitting around doing nothing would suddenly get busy. But if I was sitting down when he arrived, I made no pretense of being very busy. I didn't feel I had to prove anything, but everyone else was suddenly running around like mad.

Today, when I come into a room and see an employee suddenly getting frantically busy, I start to wonder about that employee. The question, "What are they trying to prove?" always crosses my mind.

But the next week the man who was to take my place showed up, and that was the end of the one and only job I ever had where I was working for somebody else!

CHAPTER X

Off to College and Beyond

In September of '42, I was off to the University of Massachusetts.

Coeds wore pleated skirts and baggy sweaters with bobby socks and loafers or saddle shoes, while argyle socks were the big number with young men. Everybody was jitterbugging to the Big Band sound of Tommy Dorsey, Benny Goodman, Stan Kenton, or the dreamy Glenn Miller playing "Moonlight Serenade."

The Andrews sisters brought the war to music with the "G.I. Jive" and "Boogie Woogie Bugle Boy," and I became a student at the university, a lost freshman on a campus with ten times as many students as I had known at Millis High School.

I was selected for the Army's Enlisted Reserve Corps, which let me finish my first year of college before going into the Army. It was a new experience, going from being a big fish in a small pond to a small fish in a big pond! There were new challenges and orientations, plus an exciting time of self-discovery that expanded my horizons.

At the end of my freshman year, I was picked to be part of a high I.Q. group sent to the University of New Hampshire for two weeks of special tests. That's when I learned some lessons about life and about the Army. Thirty-nine of us were selected out of the several hundred who took the tests. We were shipped to Camp Edwards down on Cape Cod where all the rich people lived. [Little did I dream that I would have a house on Cape Cod one day.] Obviously, we thought, this is going to be a snap. That was B.D.S.—Before Drill Sergeant.

The first thing we learned from our beloved Drill Sergeant upon arriving was that we were the sorriest, stupidest, no-good sons-of-bitches who have ever walked the earth. He had no hope for us or the United States of America if it was going to fight a war with the disgusting likes of us. Lesson number two was that the species Drill Sergeant cannot communicate except by screaming at the top of its lungs with the objective of shattering eardrums or spirits or penetrating brains.

Lesson three is that there is always one more line you have to stand in for whatever you want or have to do. The first day, I stood in line to eat, get a haircut, be stripped naked, inspected, dressed and yelled at.

One of these lines was at the mess hall where chow was served. It soon became clear why they called it a mess hall. They gave you a steel tray carefully divided into four compartments so as to keep four different kinds of food separate. This ingenious arrangement was instantly defeated by the orderlies in the serving line so that, by the time you got out of the chow line, all the foods, sauces, seasonings, syrups, and gravies were run together, creating a modernistic painting but not a meal.

The line for the barber also proved instructive, and I concluded that he must be the richest man on the post. He did 39 haircuts in 39 minutes and charged a dollar each. My new haircut was, admittedly, a time-saver, since I could wash my face and hair at the same time.

In the mysterious logic of the Army, we were next given a physical to see if we could qualify for the Army. This struck me as being ass-backwards, but actually it was the 39 of us who were bare-assed, buck-naked as we stood in line again. Medical corpsman attacked from all sides without warning. They performed an uncomfortable, embarrassing peek-and-poke into every orifice and appendage available for peeking or poking.

One corpsman drove—and that's the correct word—a needle into my right arm while another drove a needle into the left arm. I then took one step forward and a medic told me to "milk it down"—did this man know of my past connection with cows, milk and ice cream? —Probably just a lucky guess.

Finally, the mysterious logic of the Army became clear. They could give me a physical judging whether or not I was suitable for the Army at any point in this process, because no one has ever been known to fail the physical.

Next came the shouting supply sergeant, intent on providing us the sartorial splendor that the Army had to offer even though he only had two sizes: too big and too small. Now I never expected to look like a tailored West Point cadet, but, foolishly, I expected that at least the shoes and uniforms would halfway fit. That was one of my many mistakes before I learned about Army life.

As if by magic, our Drill Sergeant appeared on the scene and voiced the opinion that we were the slowest bunch of laggards and the sorriest bunch of sad sacks he had ever seen. If we didn't get dressed in our fatigues and haul our asses out of there in the next two minutes, we would all be on K.P. for the next two years.

Then we were outside in the sun, trying to march in a straight line, trying to keep in step, trying to carry our new clothes in both arms, and trying to listen to him tell us we were on the way to meet the best friend we would ever have in the Army while berating us for being good-for-nothing, stupid, idiotic, witless, uncoordinated, slouching, hopeless sad sacks. It occurred to me that this man had never heard of Dale Carnegie. In fact, I am sure that, if Dale Carnegie had ever met our drill sergeant, Dale would have slugged the sergeant in the mouth.

I don't know what the other 38 were fantasizing about who this best friend was going to be, but for me it would have been somebody handing me my honorable discharge papers. The best friend we would ever have was made of steel, wood, leather, and brass. It was an M-1 rifle that was nobody's best friend if he slipped when opening the beech and got his thumb caught in the damn thing, as thousands of us did.

I was not thrilled with the Army that first day. It was eleven o'clock before I literally fell onto the bed—I was too tired to get into it. I was even less thrilled when, at 5:30 a.m., the screamer was back with a voice augmented by a whistle that we thought totally superfluous.

HIT THE DECK!
Shrill whistle
HIT THE DECK!
Shrill whistle
UP AND AT 'EM
Shrill whistle
UP AND AT 'EM
Shrill whistle

I looked at him standing there at the end of the barracks and said to myself, "It's 5:30 in the morning and how the hell is he up before us with both his face and shoes bright and shining? Did he ever go to bed?"

This philosophical inquiry in my head was abruptly terminated by another of his endless references to our posteriors.

"Get your damn asses out of the sack and fall out in front of the barracks for reveille and I mean NOW!"

This wasn't the way Frank Sinatra and Gene Kelley got up in the Army in the movies I had seen. Usually, it started with a melodious bugler who would end reveille with a jazz riff, and all the gang would two-step out of the barracks and do a big dance number on the parade ground. This was just the screamer and the whistle.

We fell into line and the sergeant took roll and told us we had 20 minutes to shower and shave. Then came a quick breakfast and 30 minutes of calisthenics and we were ready to start our day.

For the next four weeks we learned to load, shoot, disassemble and assemble our best friend the M-1 and move across all kinds of terrains as if we were under enemy fire. We had to climb walls, swing on ropes across streams, jump barbed wire rolls, bayonet dummies, and then, the supreme test: crawl the infiltration course under live fire.

We had to crawl on our bellies the length of a football field under a lethal sheet of live machine gun fire. I am told that in Southern training camps crawling soldiers would encounter poisonous snakes and rise up in fear only to be hit by one of the live rounds.

Our loving drill sergeant had told us to look upon him as our mother, because it was his job to take care of us while we were away from home. It was an imagery I never could manage because I know that my mother would never make me do some of the things the drill sergeant did. Besides, she fed me better.

Anyhow, our mother away from Mother said there was absolutely no danger —long pause—as long as we kept our asses down and bodies glued to the ground. He said, just like the Southern boys with the snakes, the only time he had seen anybody get hurt was when he panicked and rose up only to be cut down.

Inquiring minds among us wanted to know why the hell we had to do this. The Sergeant had the universal answer of all drill sergeants,

"On the double. Hit the dirt and start crawling like your life depended on it, because it does."

The ground was muddy and it started out easy, crawling and using my elbows to pull myself along while my always-present M-1 was cradled in the crook of my arms. Easy, wet, and dirty, but no problem at first. Then came the machine-gun fire skimming a few inches above us. Wow! That certainly had the power to focus my mind.

I could hear those live rounds burrowing through the air just above me, punctuated with a sizzling tracer round every fifth bullet. Then the land mines started exploding in a mushroom of mud around and ahead of us, and mortar fire began cascading in our path. Considering what was happening, it occurred to me that some fool could get hurt out here.

Two thoughts crossed my busy mind, squeezed in among trying to check out where all the hazards were and figuring out how to avoid them. First, why did I need a year of college and two weeks of training to end up doing this? Second, why were soldiers belonging to the same Army I did trying to see how close they could come to killing me? I was about to die for my country and I hadn't even left Massachusetts!

Of course, the Drill Sergeant and the Army knew what they were doing, because I got mad as hell, set my jaw so hard my teeth would hurt later, and decided I would show these bastards I could take anything they could dish out. That, of course, is exactly what they wanted me to do. That was how they were training me to survive the tough times ahead of me.

Suddenly, it was over. In fact, it seemed to end surprisingly quickly after I bore down and fought my way ahead in the mud like a determined hunting dog going after a badger. The machine-gun fire stopped, the damn whistle blew, and the drill sergeant yelled—not as loudly as usual—that it was okay to stand up. We all looked like a platoon of Mud Men from Hell, but we were grinning silly grins of self congratulations. Most important, our M-1s were in great shape and ready for action.

There was a lesson learned out in the field of mud. It would serve me well in my business life to know that *sheer grit* would sometimes be the only answer for survival in the vicious world of commerce.

It was a lesson that prepared me for the most critical business battle of my life about 30 years later. One thing I will say about your enemy in war: he has a certain honesty about him that your enemy in business often doesn't have.

Your enemy in war wears a uniform that identifies him as your enemy, and he carries a gun openly. Your enemy in business often dresses and acts as if he was your friend, your buddy, or your mentor. He has deadly weapons at hand, but never lets you see them.

Both these men may destroy you the first chance they get, but I would rather face my business competitor. At least, he ain't got no bullets!

CHAPTER XI

The Army Follies

IT WAS EASY to make fun of the military in those days because of the stupid things it did. Take for example, what happened after we had been at Camp Edwards four weeks.

The Drill Sergeant called us into formation and gave us two surprising bits of information. Surprising bit of information number one was that he was proud of us! The Drill Sergeant proud of these 39 good-for-nothing, stupid, idiotic, witless, uncoordinated, slouching, hopeless sad sacks? Either we weren't hearing right or he or we had changed a lot in four weeks. I suspect it was us.

Surprising bit of information number two was the 39 of us were being shipped to Fort Ethan Allen in Vermont one week short of completing our basic training.

Well, we figured we could live with that. One week more of training at Ethan Allen and we would be as tough and ready for combat as those Green Mountain Boys led by the Revolutionary War hero, Ethan Allen.

Again, we had collectively miscalculated the Army mind. At Fort Ethan Allen, our platoon of 39 near-seasoned, almost-ready-for-prime-time-combat soldiers had to start all over again from week one. Moaning, groaning, bitching, complaining, carrying-on, and arguing—God-given rights of every

American—did no good. So we just did it, and it was a lot easier than the first time.

In the middle of the fourth week, we realized that we were trapped in a bad movie. A few years later, we would have been a perfect subject for Rod Serling's "Twilight Zone." We were called together and informed the Army was closing down Fort Ethan Allen and we were being shipped back to the University of New Hampshire for re-assignment.

By this time, we had become cocky. We looked like soldiers, we felt like soldiers, and we were soldiers! Actually, when the train dropped us at the deserted university station at 2 a.m., we felt like a bedraggled, abandoned pack of mutts.

Hey, it was war time, and we were soldiers defending our country. In the movies, we would have had a band, cheering students, and a welcoming pep rally. A cute little coed bursting out of her cheerleader's sweater would have thrown her arms around my neck, gushing about how handsome and brave I was. Instead, nothing, nil, zero, nobody, empty, zip, silence—not even anyone to tell us where we were supposed to go.

The rest of the night we spent on benches or the floor, both of which were so hard it was a relief to get up at sunrise and do calisthenics to work out our knots in front of the train station.

Then our temporary corporal dispatched a scout party of three to find whomever was in charge at the university to tell them we had arrived. Thus began ten delightful days in the limbo of a college campus stripped of most males. The only person of military rank at the university was a R.O.T.C. sergeant instructor who didn't have a clue as to why we were there or what to do with us. So we camped out waiting for him to find out.

Things were quiet at the school because it was summer, but the girls seemed to be anxious to have a man's arm to hang on to, especially an arm that was in uniform. Of course, combat veterans that we thought we were, we felt obligated to perform whatever duties in defense of our country the situation demanded.

I am a gentlemen, and gentlemen do not gossip. I am also happily married now and not stupid. So I will not detail those ten days of arduous duty. I will say that, while it was not heaven, it was pretty close. I do want to thank those lovely young ladies for being so kind to us and providing us with one additional reason to fight for democracy besides Mom and apple pie.

Finally, the gates of heaven were closed and we were pushed out, back to the station and onto a train. There we were, 39 of us on a crowded troop train chugging southward down the coast. After two days of sleeping on the floor or in luggage racks with no place to shower, we arrived at Camp Claibourne, Louisiana.

We knew we were going south because it had been getting hotter and hotter. When we got to Camp Claibourne it was hotter than hell, with humidity so high it should have been raining.

At Camp Claibourne, the saga of the 39-man platoon from the outer ozone continued. Nobody knew who we were or what we were doing there. Even so, they did find us a barracks and pointed us to the mess hall. After breakfast in the sauna they called the mess hall, we wandered around and watched trainees. They were as inept at Army drill as we had been a few months earlier, and we spent our time making remarks about how bad they were.

As good veteran soldiers, we scouted out the situation and immediately made ourselves comfortable. The barracks were built a couple of feet off the ground, as are many southern buildings, so as to allow air to circulate underneath and cool the place and sometimes, because of occasional flooding in the area.

Well, we crawled under the barracks and found it was cool compared to being out there in the sunlight. That's how we spent the first day. That's how we spent the second day. By the second day, books and checkers appeared and we only came out for meals and to sleep in our beds at night. That's how we spent the third day.

"WHAT IN THE HELL DO YOU BASTARDS THINK YOU ARE DOING?"

I jumped up so hard I hit my head on the underside of the barracks floor. The voice was not the familiar screaming of our original Drill Sergeant. This was more of a bellow—a deep-throated cannon roar. A regimental cannon roar used to address larger groups than a sergeant normally does. The roaring sound was all the more intimidating, since it seemed to be coming from the center of a beet-red officer's face about two feet from my ear. Then, of course, came the ever-present reference to that part of the human anatomy with which the Army seemed obsessed, "GET YOUR NO GOOD ASSES OUT OF THERE ON THE DOUBLE."

The bellower with the voice that almost broke my eardrum was a major, and he made our drill sergeant screamer seem like a nice guy.

We stood at attention as he paced back and forth, livid with rage and demonstrating an extraordinary talent. For twenty minutes, choice rhetorical prose spat out of his face like machine-gun bullets, echoing off the barracks walls and spilling out all over the dusty, hot, bleached parade ground. The whole time the man never took a breath.

Naturally, other trainees around the area were taking all this in, some of them free to relax while on a short break. But in all the embarrassment I was feeling about being made a spectacle of in public, I became aware of a new perception. I was about to learn another lesson about life and I was still in my teens.

Instead of mocking us or making sarcastic remarks about our predicament, I sensed the other trainees sympathized with us. Some of them gave us the clenched-fist-hang-tough-brother sign. It was a brotherhood of the miserable. I and the rest of us realized we had much in common with those boys from the South, and I vowed never to make fun of anyone again.

The lesson is that we are all just people, and each of us has our shortcomings which tend to balance off the shortcomings of the other guy. To survive in the Army, on the battlefield, in the world or in life, we have to stick together or each one of us is lost. Even star basketball or baseball players such as the ones with whom I do Dairy Mart television commercials couldn't be stars if all those other guys weren't backing them up.

There could be no star without a supporting team. If you doubt that, consider this: somebody once dreamed up the idea of All-Star games in football, baseball, and basketball. When you put all these stars together on the same team, you should have one dynamite team—right? Wrong! Everybody knows that All-Star teams turn out to be pretty mediocre. There is a place for stars in every calling, but they are adrift and powerless without the help and cooperation of the rest of us.

What happened next to us—"The 39ers"—was something unbelievable. It's true because I could never make this up, but it certainly was bizarre to 39 college kids from New England.

The bellow-voiced major took us to his boss, a colonel. The colonel calmly ordered that we be marched as a unit for 48 hours straight without stopping except for food. Think about it. The colonel's specific order was, "Take these clowns out and march them for 48 hours straight."

The major rounded up half-a-dozen sergeants and a jeep. The sergeants traded off every two hours marching us through the humid heat. This was accompanied by their incessant cursing of us for causing them all this trouble. Hell, it wasn't our idea, it was the colonel's.

The sun went down. The sun came up. The sun went down. The sun came up. Finally, when the sun started down on the second day, the march was over. We had only stopped for 30 minutes each at breakfast, lunch, and dinner. When it was over, the sergeants begrudgingly admitted that we were 39 tough soldiers. More important, each of us felt a pride in what we had done together. We had a bond of shared adversity that would always be with us, even if we never saw each other again.

The colonel finally realized that we were wrongly assigned to Camp Claibourne. He corrected that mistake by sending us to Fort Benning, Georgia, for 13 weeks of O.C.S./A.S.T.P. [Officer's Candidate School/Army Specialized Training Program] basic training. This was the third time we had had basic training, and we were *really* trained. Then the Army broke us up which was too bad. We would have been a great team had we continued together on the rest of our active duty.

However, all of the 39ers were A.S.T.P. and assigned to different colleges throughout the country. I went to Johns Hopkins University in Baltimore.

After two semesters in 24 weeks, I ended up assigned to the 84th Infantry Division as a private. I was a well-schooled and well-trained private, but a private nonetheless. After filling all the vacant slots the 84th had for privates, the Army gave us leave before sending us to Fort Dix, New Jersey, for overseas assignment.

All the time I was away in college and in the Army, I dreamed about returning to the love of my life, the woman who would be my wife, my Mimi.

After the grueling experience of basic training, I eagerly came home on leave. One of the first things I was going to do was call Mimi who, by that time, was at the University of Alabama—waiting to hear from me, I was positive.

When I told my mother I was going to call Mimi, she got a funny look on her face such as I had not seen before and I knew something was wrong. I picked up the phone anyhow and heard Mother say, "I don't think you better call her."

"What do you mean?" I asked, suddenly sensing a sick feeling coming over me as the answer came to me with stupefying clarity. I knew what she meant, but I didn't want to hear it.

"Well, I hear she is engaged to someone else," were the exact words in all the world that I did not want to hear from Mother or anybody else.

Crushed but unbelieving, I had to call her for that final humiliation that all lovers require at the end. After telling me how she had not been sure I loved her or known if I would ever be back, she admitted she was engaged and "hoped I would understand."

Well, I didn't understand, but was too proud to beg. So, I said, "Sure," and hung up heartbroken. It was over. How could it be over? Still, it was. My great high school love was no more. You know how egos, especially at that age, can get in the way of life? I felt terrible and knew that I would wither away or deliberately die a heroic death in battle and then Mimi would be sorry. Well, it would serve her right.

To my breathless amazement, I actually survived, and in the process learned another important lesson, namely, some of the best things that happen to you in life are the things you didn't get.

After this heartbreak, I went on to Fort Dix. From there we knew we were going overseas and would probably go right into combat, because D-Day, the invasion of Europe, had been June 6th, and it was now September. Casualties had been heavy, and the front line troops had been fighting hard all summer. Now they needed fresh troops and guess who that was going to be?

After 10 days of waiting, we boarded a British ship named "Sterling Castle," which turned out to be neither sterling nor a castle.

I wasn't too worried about U-Boats at this point, because the Navy had just about whipped that menace. Even so, after 24 hours at sea we collided with another ship—a Navy cruiser—and all of a sudden the troop ship "Sterling Castle" was taking on water—fast.

Coming about at full speed, the ship headed for land as fast as it could. I was thinking, get me to Terra Firma, and the firma it is, the less the terra there is. Luckily, we got back all right. We went back to Fort Dix while the Castle went to the Brooklyn Naval Yard for a quick patch job.

That meant we all got a one-day pass to go into town until another troop ship arrived. Little did I know that it would turn out to be another bloody encounter because I was a Jew.

CHAPTER XII

Joining the Crusade in Europe

WE WERE ABOUT to join Eisenhower's great Crusade For Freedom in Europe that would allow all men to live in peace, freedom and equality, when First Sergeant Koehler in the bunk below said loudly, "I hear you kikes had a big party last night."

This from a sergeant in the great Crusade for Freedom? I somehow thought the days of derogatory names like "kikes" were behind me now that I was in the United States Army, but I was obviously wrong.

What was particularly galling about the remark is not only the word, but the insult to my religion. It happened that our one-day pass coincided with Yom Kippur, and several of us of the Jewish faith had headed for the synagogue and prayed with people who took us into their homes to break our fasts after more than 24 hours of not eating.

The next day we were back at Fort Dix boarding another troopship, with the bunks stacked six high and only a little over a foot between every two bunks. It was not a place for anyone with claustrophobia.

I grabbed a top bunk and settled down to rest and think over my last night ashore in prayer and about the possibility that I might never be coming home. I wasn't worried, just realistic, and it was comforting that I had had the chance to observe

Yom Kippur in the traditional way on what might be my last time in my country.

Then the sarcastic racial and religious slur spoiled it for me.

I knew that Koehler, the top kick, was regular Army, and I had long suspected that his I.Q. matched his hat size, but I wasn't prepared for that remark. It seemed so mean-spirited, so uncalled for, so vicious at a time when we were all supposed to be buddies about to enter battle.

"What did you say?"

"You heard what I said. I hear you kikes had a party in town last night."

The Germans and Russians were in a death struggle before Stalingrad, Paris had been liberated, and MacArthur was about to wade through the surf and return to the Philippines—and I was jammed into a tiny troop ship compartment at Fort Dix, New Jersey, confronting a jerk who represented the opposite of everything all those people were fighting and dying for. Unfortunately, we can't always pick our times and places.

Something snapped, and I swung over the side of my bunk, grabbed the anti-Semitic bastard's hair and began beating his head against the steel railing of his bunk. Instantly, guys were all over us pulling us apart.

That day I saw a violent side of myself that I didn't know was buried deep in my psyche. What surprised me most was that I knew I would have continued to hammer that son-of-a-bitch's head until it split wide open if they hadn't grabbed me.

I had committed a breach of the Military Code—assaulting a superior non-commissioned officer—and could have been court-martialed, but Kike-Hater Koehler knew the Army way and said nothing. There had been too many witnesses to his Jew-baiting, and a charge against me would have hurt him more than me because he was staying in the Army. I and a couple million others were getting out just as soon as we could. He would just lay in wait for a chance to get me later.

Our troop ship was nearing England when Koehler got his chance, or so he thought. Here again my biggest ally was his I.Q., which, on a hot day, might match his age. He got a request for a volunteer from our company to do "red ball" duty as soon as we landed. Dim-bulb that he was, he assumed red ball duty meant rushing immediately into combat. Guess who he "volunteered" for the job? His old Jewish friend from Millis, Massachusetts.

In fact, the assignment was to drive a truck in the Red Ball express, rushing supplies to ships waiting to sail for France. I spent my days shuttling back and forth from supply depots twenty miles inland to the ships in port. It was a choice job, and I owed it all to Koehler. The biggest thing I had ever driven before was my little peddler's truck, but bluff is part of survival in the Army and a lot of other places, too. So I swung into the cab of that 2 1/2 ton Army truck, hauling a 40-foot trailer behind me, and started rolling down the highway.

Then came the day we loaded ourselves onto the ships and headed for the French shore ten miles—ten turbulent, rough, stomach-tossing miles away. We almost didn't make it. Caught by a storm in the English Channel, our ship couldn't land in France and couldn't turn back to England. So we sat trapped like seasick children, bobbing up and down and sideways in all directions, for ten horrible days. I pitched, dipped, rolled, and banged, with a lot of my buddies hanging over the side. All we had to eat for those ten days was canned beans. And my mother wondered why I didn't like beans anymore when I came home!

As we finally edged toward the French shore, one of the barges next to us, which was also loaded with trucks, suddenly split open as if hit by a cleaver from heaven and sank before anybody could move to get off. It sent a shudder through us to know how mindlessly and quickly death could come out here so far away from home.

My tour with the Red Ball express ended about three weeks later, when the 84th had crossed the Channel to join us. I was then back to my old outfit and my friend the bigoted first sergeant.

We moved right into combat, and the first day he got shot in the leg and got shipped stateside [some thought the wound was self-inflicted]. That was just as well. He was regular Army and operated best stateside, where his courage would never be seriously challenged and he could bully draftees and green recruits. He didn't last 24 hours in combat and, frankly, that was fine with me.

Then I got my first taste of combat. They needed "volunteers," and our squad leader, Sergeant Jim Cooney, pointed and said, "you, you, you, you, and you." I was the third you.

We went down to a little barricaded bunker where there were tables covered with maps like linen tablecloths. Naturally, into this tiny, safe room were jammed officers: a captain, a major, and a colonel. They told us how brave we were and how much they appreciated our volunteering for this dangerous mission.

I'm saying to myself, "What volunteering? What dangerous mission? I didn't ask to go anyplace. I'd rather stay here in the bunker with you guys." I'm saying nothing to everyone else, nothing because that's what privates do when colonels are playing colonel and using pointers on the map before us.

"Gentlemen, you are right here."

He was a chubby fellow with a fine, pencil mustache carefully waxed so that it was like a cat's whiskers and vibrated when he talked. He might have stepped right off the parade ground at West Point.

I suspected we were in deep trouble when he called us "gentlemen." Then he confirmed it.

"And here," he continued, moving his pointer, "is a pillbox that must be knocked out."

That word "pillbox" did it for sure. To women a pillbox is a cute little hat worn by Jackie Kennedy Onassis. To men in combat, it is a strongly fortified machine-gun and cannon nest.

Anytime a colonel calls five privates and a sergeant "gentlemen," you know he wants something big, like your blood. Combine that with "pillbox," and you are talking about one of the easiest ways in the world to lose blood—your blood, not the colonel's.

"This one pillbox is holding up an entire Army from advancing. It is strategically located with two heavy machine guns and a gun big enough to knock out tanks. We cannot call in artillery fire, because there are troops to the right and the left and in front of the pillbox. So there is a danger of our own troops being killed by friendly fire."

What I was worried about was some of our own troops being killed by hostile fire—us! Again, the logic of the military mind escaped me. I thought to myself, "Well, colonel, you shouldn't have our troops so close to the pillbox. Why not order a temporary withdrawal of the endangered troops back a hundred yards or so and then call in artillery fire to knock out the pillbox? Makes a lot more sense than sending the six of us up there to knock out a pillbox that your entire Army can't handle."

The colonel continued in his most official tone, which implied that the fate of the Western World depended on us.

"It is now twenty hundred hour. You will leave here at oh-three hundred hour and you should be there by oh-four hundred hour. We want to see you back here at oh-six hundred hour at the latest. That will give you an hour to look the pillbox over, come up with a plan to take it out, take it out, and return to these headquarters."

Then came the dramatic pause, the forward lean to stare right into our eyes to communicate the gravity of the moment and the mission, "The fate of a lot of lives is now in your hands. Good luck!"

Right out of a John Wayne movie! Complete with shifting the blame from him to us in advance if it didn't work. Sounded exciting except that this was no movie and someone could get hurt. Badly.

Next came the scene right out of "All Quiet On The Western Front," just before the line of infantrymen go over the top into the withering gun fire.

We all took out our wallets and started exchanging pictures and things like that.

"If anything happens to me, will you send this to my mother?"

"See that my wife gets this."

That's when the voice of sanity overrode the B-movie dialog. Sergeant Cooney snapped us back, "Listen you guys, I don't want any more of this shit. Each of you is an excellent rifleman. Those goddamned Jerrys are afraid of us. They know we are going to take them out eventually. All of you guys are coming back. You are the best fighters we have for this job and we know you can do it.

"I picked each one of you because you are good and because I have faith in you. So put that stuff back in your pockets and try to get a little shuteye. I want you to go in there with clear heads. The krauts will be asleep. Surprise them and kick the living shit out of them and everyone of you, and, I mean EVERY one of you will be coming back a hero."

What an inspiring speech! Obviously it inspired me, because I remember it very clearly today, 48 years later. I also remember Sergeant Jim Cooney and the lesson he helped me learn about success.

The lesson is teamwork. It goes back to what I said about sports stars being nothing without a team to back them up. None of us could have taken that pillbox alone. But as a team —as a team with a plan—we could do it.

I may have been the boss at Dairy Mart, but I had a team of key people upon whom I depended. I also listened. I listened to them, and I listened to the troops in the field, and I listened to our customers.

Any business executive who thinks his company is a success entirely because of what he does has an ego problem for openers. That ego problem will, in turn, lead to a lot of other problems more serious for him, his company, his employees, and his stockholders. An executive must provide direction and leadership, but, if he is smart, he will "work with" and "listen to" his team.

Jimmy Cooney was a great leader. A helluva lot better leader than the wax-mustache colonel safe in the bunker.

It was dark as hell and sloppy cold when we crept across what they called No-Man's Land. I thought to myself, "If this is No-Man's Land, what the hell am I doing here?"

We had to be careful of ditches, water holes, barbed wire, assorted debris, land mines, and other hazards as we picked our way toward the pillbox chiseled out of the side of this small mountain between France and Germany—probably part of the Siegfried Line.

We had muffled everything we had that was metal to avoid any clanking sounds, including taking off our metal helmets, and blackened our faces and anything else that would reflect the light of the full moon. We moved quickly, but carefully, to case the pillbox.

The arrangement was lethally simple. The Germans had built the gun emplacement into the side of the mountain with two-foot-thick reinforced concrete walls, a steel trap door on top, and three gun slits in the front, each one closed with its own steel shutter. The smaller ones for the machine guns were on each side, and the bigger one for the antitank cannon was in the middle. Its simplicity also made it a tough target.

We quickly pulled back and huddled over what to do, talking in hushed tones and hoping that no one inside the gun emplacement heard anything suspicious outside. We figured most of the Germans would be asleep with one guy on sentry duty. We assumed that even the sleeping Germans could be awakened into action in less than a minute if we set off the alarm by being heard or seen.

In the huddle, Cooney directed the meeting and told us what to do. It was a good feeling to have this take-charge guy leading us.

"It's not going to take an hour to knock those bastards out of that pillbox. Here is how we're going to do it:

"I'll swing way around and come back along the ridge of the hill until I am right on top of the pillbox. Meanwhile, you guys go back to where we were. I want the BAR [Browning Automatic Rifle] man [that was me] to zero in on the center slit. Two of you get set to lay down fire on the right slit and the other two on the left slit.

"I want all five of you spread out with 25 feet between you so they'll think there's several times our number firing at them. When they open the slits, I want a lot of dirt kicked up so they can't see what's going on.

"I'm counting on one of them being stupid enough to open the steel door on the top to see what's happening. The second that damn door comes up, a hand grenade is going in. Any questions? Any better ideas?"

Minutes later we were all in position, fanned out in front of the dreaded pillbox, and Jim was on top of the emplacement waving us the signal to start firing.

It happened just as Jim had predicted, except that the Germans started shooting as soon as we did. They must have been really light sleepers, because all I know is I fired a couple of bursts with my BAR and the air was instantly filled with flying lead. It was just like crawling on my belly back at the Camp Edwards infiltration course except these guys meant to kill me.

Suddenly, I felt a hot sting on the side of my head, but I paid little attention to it. We had important things to accomplish.

In the next few seconds, that bad news was followed by two happy developments. I could immediately tell I was not hit badly, and the counter barrage stopped as someone inside did open the trap door and Cooney's grenade rolled into the pillbox and decimated those poor bastards inside.

There were a couple of minor wounds on the other guys, and mine turned out to be a small piece of shrapnel, but Cooney was right and that made it all okay. We had taken the pillbox and marched back into camp that morning with pride.

We all got the Bronze Star for bravery in action. It really should have been for brains in action.

Unfortunately, Jim Cooney was buried alive in a foxhole by an incoming artillery shell a few weeks later. Even when I knew in my head he was dead, I refused to accept it in my heart for a long, long time. I think the reason that I am alive today is the way Jim Cooney handled the attack on that pillbox. He was a leader who could think and who never asked anyone of us in his squad to do a dirty job that he wouldn't do himself. There weren't a lot of men like him—certainly not among those officers in the bunker. I'm just sorry he didn't make it and sorry that I never had a chance to pay him back. What a contrast to Sergeant Koelher sitting on his butt back in the States.

Strange how things work out in war. Some die. Some live. Some are maimed and should have died, but are doomed to live.

By the winter of 1944-45 I was acting platoon sergeant. The war had transformed from a triumphant roll up of German defenses in mid-1944 to a stalemate by the winter of 1944-45. The war had come down to what our Commander-in-Chief, General Dwight Eisenhower, characterized as "the dirtiest kind of infantry slugging."

Soon after I arrived in France and about the time we knocked out the pillbox, Eisenhower faced one of the most important decisions of his Crusade in Europe, one that would decide how soon the war would end and how soon this native of Millis would go home to his mother's farm house and good cooking. Of course, Ike didn't consult me on this one, but it sure meant a lot to me.

Ike had enough gasoline to unleash Patton's 3rd Armored

Joining the Crusade in Europe   81

Division to punch into Germany and across the Rhine and on to Berlin. Or, he could give the gasoline to Montgomery to push ahead and capture Calais, Dunkirk, and Antwerp.

Montgomery got the gas and, in typical Montgomery fashion dedicated to all show and no go, wasted it with a paratroop drop on the Dutch city of Arnheim, where the Germans were alerted in advance and waiting to massacre the parachutists as they hung helplessly in the air.

That was all high-level and far away from Acting Sergeant Charlie Nirenberg, but it was the reason I and my men were slogging through the cold snow entering the little German town of Aachen, which was the ancient capitol used by Charlemagne—the ancient French version of the name Charles.

My squad was on the move. We were dirty, tired, cold, and not terribly interested in the historical background of Aachen. What we were interested in were the simple comforts of life that, in combat, become the outrageous luxuries of life.

It had been three weeks since we had eaten a hot meal, so I shot two rabbits and two chickens that we carried with us until we bedded down for the night in the cellar of a German family's house.

I told the woman of the house to fix us a stew out of the rabbits and the chickens. I spoke enough German to get by, and the family had some potatoes and onions and some cabbage. Things were looking great until this captain stopped by.

"What the hell do you think you're doing?"

"Hey, these guys haven't had a hot meal in three weeks and these people are cooking one for us."

"Are you crazy or something? You can't trust these people. They're liable to poison you."

"Well, if they poison us, they're going to poison themselves first because they're going to taste what they cook before we eat it."

With that, the captain exploded. He began to rant and threaten me with court-martial and a lot of other bull. After my time in combat, I really didn't care.

"Where do they get these guys they make into officers?" I thought to myself. "They are always giving me a hard time and acting stupid."

I think the captain sensed my frame of mind and wisely decided to leave. Too bad. If he had been the officer and gentlemen his commission proclaimed him to be, he could have eaten some damn good stew with us.

In the supreme irony of this incident, the careful captain got himself blown to hell a few hours later when he opened a booby-trapped door.

I always made the Germans open doors first or touch anything suspicious. I figured they weren't any more anxious to die than I was. The same thing was true of poisoning. That night, we enjoyed a hot meal and lived. The next day, the captain did something foolish and died.

In Aachen it was just as Ike said it would be. We tried to push forward, but the Germans were dug in and had us pinned down with hostile fire. We were miserable—wet, cold, tired, and scared. What a terrible thing to endure. It was two weeks before we broke out and started moving again.

I suspect that German resistance got tougher and tougher as we moved forward. We were in Germany now, not somebody else's country that had been occupied by the Germans. Aachen, in fact, was the first German town the Allies had captured in this Crusade.

While we were pinned down by the Germans in Aachen and I crouched down in this idiotic two-man foxhole half-filled with water with my buddy Steve, I dreamed of how nice it would be to be sitting in a dry foxhole filled with hay.

Louis Nirenberg in Hamburg, Germany, before boarding the ship to America (1912).

(Left to right) My sister, Ann; my mother; my brother, Morris; and, my brother, Barney before coming to America.

My father (far right) in tailor shop in Boston with his brother, Charlie (second from right).

My high school graduation picture when I was already in the ice cream business.

Me and classmates at elementary school in Millis, Massachusetts.

With my buddies from the 84th Regiment in Europe.

Home on leave from the Army in front of our house in Millis.

My basic training group at Fort Benning, Georgia.

The family at dinner after I left the Army. (Left to right, clockwise around the table) My brother, Morris; Morris' wife, Lorry; my brother-in-law, Meyer Cherkas; my sister, Ann; Me; my wife, Jan; my kid brother, Joe; Joe's first wife Muriel; Barney's wife, Rose; my brother, Barney; and, my mother (circa 1950-51).

Jan and I courting in the ice cream truck (1948).

Our wedding picture, 1949.

The Snow White Princess Contest winner, Carla Rota, and her court, along with Mayor Daniel B. Brunton of Springfield and Miss Massachusetts of 1956.

An early Dairy Mart store (1958).

The Snow White Ice Cream plant I built by hand in 1952 in Springfield, Massachusetts.

(Left to right) My mother-in-law, Avis Shamitz; me; my wife, Jan; my mother, Sarah; and, my father-in-law, Morris Shamitz.

An early Dairy Mart Milk Mobile truck.

Princess Ice Cream Parlour team, me; manager, Ken Murphy; and, supervisor, Walter Andrews.

Daughter Sandi's high school graduation picture.

My son, Larry, in front of the Dairy Mart Farm Store.

My daughter, Pam, on graduation from high school.

*Giant executives in a Princess Ice Cream Parlour.
(Left to right) Ted Kaufman, Charlie Nirenberg, Al Bloom and, Ben Lieberman.*

Me arriving in a pony cart to dedicate new Enfield plant (1975).

CHAPTER XIII

The Crusade Won and the Price Paid

I SPOTTED A barn off to the right in a little grove of trees. It was about halfway between where we were and where the Germans were and didn't seem occupied. I figured I would sneak over there after dark, get a bunch of hay, and bring it back to soak up all the damn water we were standing in.

When darkness fell, I crawled on my belly through the sloppy mud to the barn, getting filthier and wetter along the way. Sure enough, there was lots of loose hay in the barn. I loaded my arms with both hay and my best friend, my M-1 rifle, and crawled back to safety. The only problem was that I was losing hay as I went, leaving a trail behind me and arriving back at the foxhole with only a handful of hay. My foxhole buddy, Steve, tried the same thing, with the same result.

Ultimately, the whole thing was a worthless effort, because we never brought enough hay back while we exposed ourselves to being caught out in the open by the Germans and perforated with lead.

With the luck of the young, we survived, and I later used this story as a lesson to my Dairy Mart employees. We can compare the gross profit with the bundle of hay I started out with at that German barn. By the time you get to the net profit it is like crawling through the mud and losing most of your hay along the way. At Dairy Mart we start out with a gross profit bundle of 35 percent, but by the time we get back to safety, we only have a few straws left—in the case of Dairy Mart, 1 percent.

That time in the snowy, wet, cold, muddy, lonely German countryside filled with people looking to kill us, I learned something else that I would later use as part of my business success at Dairy Mart.

On Thanksgiving Day, we were pinned down and miserable with morale lower than a snake's belly—a freezing cold snake's belly. Oh, sure, we were alive and we had memories of past Thanksgiving feasts at home, but today it was going to be K-Rations for dinner.

Then we heard sporadic gunfire. A few bursts, then nothing, then a few more bursts and then nothing again. This went on for about ten minutes. We couldn't figure out what was going on, but the living never stick their heads out of a foxhole out of sheer curiosity.

All of a sudden, our platoon leader, Lieutenant Kohr, was lowering a bucket of turkey and cranberry sauce into our foxhole and whispering loudly, "Happy Thanksgiving, fellows. Help yourself."

As much as we disliked a lot of the officers, here was one, Lieutenant Kohr, who genuinely cared about his men. He risked himself to go from foxhole to foxhole and see that the men of his unit got a little turkey and cranberry sauce. For me it was the best Thanksgiving turkey I ever tasted before or since.

I thought about Lt. Kohr a few Thanksgivings ago when I had a trade show coming up with our store managers. I told them the story of Lt. Kohr and how he cared enough to bring turkey to the troops at their foxhole and that Dairy Mart cared enough for them in the same way and would be bringing turkeys to their foxhole [their homes] that year as a symbol of caring for our good people. It was very effective!

Soon after that Thanksgiving, the 84th broke through the German lines and got moving again, but we didn't reckon with the Nazi's Christmas Surprise. None of us would have wished for it under our tree, but it came anyhow, as dawn broke over the snow-laden fields and ice-crusted forests deep in the Ardennes in front of us. It was a huge counter-attack of several thousand tanks, hundreds of thousands of German infantrymen, and a couple thousand planes. With slashing surprise, the Battle of the Bulge hit us.

The overcast, rainy, snowy skies sealed the place off from help from the air and, for six days and nights, it became a toe-to-toe infantry slug-fest.

The American situation looked desperate and the German commander demanded surrender, to which General Tony McAuliffe gave the one word answer that would emblazon his name in military history—NUTS. Coincidentally, the skies cleared the next day. Allied planes roared in to help and the crisis was over.

By April 18th, most German resistance was over except in a few diehard pockets. The unconditional surrender was signed at the town of Reims on May 7th.

The war was over for me. I came out of it with a small scar on my head and a case of trench foot from standing in foxhole water for weeks. A lot of my buddies weren't so lucky. They were the real heroes who never came back.

By the end of the war, 400,000 young Americans had given their lives so those of us who remain can be free. I am mindful of that sacrifice, because it was made by a lot of men I knew and whose faces I can still see in my mind's eye.

CHAPTER XIV

A New Industry That Would Make Me Rich

MEANWHILE THINGS WERE happening around the country that would make it possible for the newly discharged veteran, Charlie Nirenberg, to become rich beyond his wildest dreams.

The people responsible for these developments were people I would never meet or know, but I was able to build on what they started. I took what they began and made it work for me many years later.

For example, in the mid-1920s two profound changes swept across America:

1. Great mobility because of cars.
2. Busier life style focused outside the home.

Cars began as playthings for the rich, but soon everybody wanted one. Henry Ford succeeded in producing a reliable Flivver at a price ordinary people could afford. However, the biggest obstacle to the sale of cars was the lack of hard-surfaced roads. Ordinary roads were so bad that it was hard to go more than 20 miles per hour and potholes and ruts produced at least one flat tire for about every 100 miles of driving.

Then, politicians discovered that taxpayers would support money for hard surfaced roads, and the paving of America began. With it came the flood of automobile owners, until by 1925 Henry Ford and other auto makers had sold over 15 million cars, and car-based businesses such as super markets like Piggly-Wiggly and Stop-and-Shop blossomed.

At the same time, women became more liberated and freed from home, with a growing number of them entering the workplace. This meant women had less time and wanted more labor-saving devices at home, as well as packaged, precooked foods. And something was happening in Texas that would directly affect the Nirenberg family in Massachusetts.

In those days, ice was considered a public utility and a necessity for preserving food. There were many ice manufacturing and sales stores or docks around the country including several in Oak Cliff, Texas, a small suburb of Dallas.

There Jodie Thompson, a young man who would seriously touch my life even though I never met him, lived next door to J.O. Jones, general manager of the Consumers Ice Company. Jodie worked for Jones at the ice company all through school at Oak Cliff High and the University of Texas at Austin. He loaded ice wagons, cleaned stables, groomed horses and helped build stores and plants.

He fell in love with Margaret Philp but his $150 a month salary wasn't enough for them to get married. So in the summer of 1924, he proposed a new idea to the conservative J.O. Jones. Jodie wanted to sell ice-cold watermelon from the Consumer Ice docks. Jones didn't think it would work, but he was willing to give it a shot. He let Jodie go ahead on his own with his own money. By the end of the summer, Jodie had made $2,300, and he and Margaret got married.

Later, Consumer Ice was bought by the Southland Ice Company and John "Uncle Johnny" Jefferson Green operated one of the retail docks acquired by the new Southland Ice company. This was at 12th and Edgefield Streets in Oak Cliff. Uncle Johnny made it a point to talk with and listen to his customers.

This, incidentally, is what I have done all my life as part of my Nirenberg Method of business success. It is critical to know your customers—what they think and what they like and dislike. For some strange reason, lots of businesses in this country today are in deep trouble because the big shots at the top are too arrogant to follow this fundamental rule.

Uncle Johnny was open seven days a week, 16 hours a day, while regular grocery stores kept much shorter hours. His customers complained they didn't have any place to get basic necessities when the regular grocery stores were closed. Some said it would be nice if Uncle Johnny sold more than just ice.

He talked it over with his wife and, entirely on his own and out of his own pocket, began stocking bread, milk, and eggs on the side. The idea was an immediate success, and he soon had to add shelves to carry more items.

Excited about his success, Uncle Johnny talked to Jodie about it at Southland headquarters. He told Jodie he wanted to stock about 12 items—milk, eggs, bread, cigarettes and a few canned items and keep the dock open during the winter when the ice business was dead. He wanted Jodie to foot the bills and promised he would come in to the office in the spring and settle up with Jodie. Jodie loved new ideas. He agreed to the concept and promptly forgot about Uncle Johnny.

One day about this same time the Southland president, Claude Dawley, was on an inspection tour with one of his operators, Ernest Laubscher. At one of the ice docks run by Laubscher, Dawley watched a customer drive in, buy a bottle of milk and a loaf of bread, and drive out without buying any ice.

Laubscher explained that he was experimenting with an idea for year-around operation. Usually, when winter came, the ice business closed down until the next spring. If he could stay open all year, he reasoned, it would be more efficient. Even at that embryonic point in the development of the convenience store concept, the two main commodities provided the customer were convenience and time saving.

A few days later, as he had promised months before, Uncle Johnny showed up at Southland headquarters in the Santa Fe Building of downtown Dallas and handed Jodie $1,000 in cash as Southland's share of Uncle Johnny's profits.

That immediately convinced Claude Dawley and Jodie Thompson of the soundness of the convenience store concept.

Of course, not everybody saw the new concept as a good thing. For one thing, churches and competitors didn't like

Southland's stores being open on Sunday and late at night. That was being too convenient for the public and unfair competition for God and other grocery stores.

The public reaction was to swarm into these handy new outlets that allowed people to buy necessities without wasting a lot of time and without a lot of hassle.

The most serious opposition, however, didn't come from God, but rather a major grocery chain that was a big customer of Southland Ice. The chain threatened to cancel its ice orders if Southland didn't get out of the grocery business even in the limited way it was operating.

A parallel to this would later happen in my own business, involving Irving Feinstein, who ran Grower's Outlet stores, one of my oldest and best wholesale ice cream customers. He thought I was a competitive threat to his grocery chain and wanted me to get out of the convenience store business. Obviously, I didn't.

The Southland chain called itself Tote'm Stores until after World War II, when Jodie Thompson, then in charge of the operation, approved an advertising agency's plan to consolidate all their stores under the lucky name 7-11, with universal operating hours from 7 a.m. to 11 p.m.

Back in Millis, I was getting out of the Army and getting into some more important things in my life.

CHAPTER XV

The Brothers Nirenberg

At the beginning of 1946, brother Charlie had been through the war, while brother Morris had been able to put over 100,000 dollars in the bank.

After several years in the U.S. Army I finally got what I had yearned for during those hazardous times, a piece of paper saying I was honorably discharged from the U.S. Army. It was on January 27, 1946, that I left the Army. My grateful government said I was entitled to draw $20 a week for the next 52 weeks until I found a job. Of course, I wasn't planning on going to work for anybody, because my brief taste of that at the Herman Shoe Company had soured me on working for other people.

A perfect role model was my older brother Morris. Eleven years older than I, he had flunked the Army physical. By the time I got back from saving the world for democracy, Morris had saved over $100,000 by selling ice cream. In 1946, $100,000 was a fortune. For most people it's a lot of money even today.

I didn't resent his getting rich, but it did ease my mind about getting paid $20 a week for doing nothing. My plan was to return to the University of Massachusetts in September and just loaf on the $20 a week until then. Two million other veterans were doing exactly the same thing and would soon be jammed onto college campuses across the country.

My plan had a fatal flaw: the Nirenberg adrenaline. By the end of four weeks I was chomping at the bit to be building a business. I couldn't contain myself any more. For the next nine weeks I collected my $20 while I got ready to get going, to start moving, to commence building, to be working—this is a Nirenberg characteristic over which I have no control.

Then Morris said,

"Charlie, let's go into business together. We'll be partners and you can make some real money."

The timing was perfect for my mood, and it sounded mighty good to me. I got a G.I. business loan for $4,000, Morris put in his $4,000, and we opened a small ice cream manufacturing plant in Medway, Golden Meadow Ice Cream.

Overnight, my days of doing nothing turned into being up at 6 a.m. distributing ice cream to peddlers until noon, eating a fast sandwich and distributing ice cream to wholesale accounts and stores until 6 p.m., 30 minutes for dinner, and over to the plant to make ice cream for the next day until midnight.

With the day's work out of the way, of course, nothing would do but for a young war veteran cum business tycoon to go out with his friend Fred Yonda to pick up a couple of beers and a couple of girls.

Only the young, fit, eager, and foolish can go at that kind of pace for long, but I learned every facet of the business and recommend it to any young person starting a business.

You have to know your business inside out if you are going to grow. That way you will know what to expect of your employees once the business expands and you hire people to help you. Sometimes an employer demands too much and sometimes too little, unless he has done the job himself and can fairly judge what's involved.

An 18-hour work day was standard for me, but Morris was not much for such long hours. I soon found out why and it worried me. Morris was sick with something called ileitis and had about five years to live according to the doctors.

He was my brother, and I couldn't ask him to work as hard as I did since his sickness bothered me. First my father with cancer and now Morris with ileitis. Did this mean something genetic in our family? I never wanted to talk about it to anybody, but I had it on my mind and it affected some of my decisions.

Morris was a good businessman, and I learned a lot from him that would be valuable to me in the years to come, no matter what happened to Morris.

However, there was another problem inside my head. I still wanted to go back to school and finish my education. Education was very important to me and, with the G.I. Bill, Uncle Sam was making it much easier for me. In spite of my intentions, Morris didn't believe I would go back to school in the fall and neither did my mother.

"How can you think of leaving poor Morris?" she would ask me. I was old enough to understand now how parents use guilt as a lever for what they think is the good of the total family. Guilt as a way of getting children to do what parents think they ought to do. Of course, children use guilt on parents and parents do the same on children. My mother was happy seeing her two boys working side by side in a prospering business. She also knew Morris was sick and needed me.

Well, the stubborn Nirenberg streak surfaced. I showed them all by returning to the university that fall in spite of a terrible scene with Morris calling me a quitter and making me feel I had betrayed the family. Wow! That was a heavy burden of guilt for everybody to dump on Charlie. Obviously, I still remember it. The only good part about it is that it may have made me more understanding occasionally about the dreams and aspirations of my own kids and why they wanted to leave the nest and not come into Dairy Mart.

> *I left Springfield because I had a need to make a life for myself. If I lived in Springfield, people used to call me Little Miss Dairy Mart. That was my title. I had a need to have my own identity and, for a while, I'm not sure Dad understood that.*
>
> —My daughter Pam

When I got to Amherst, my mind was not 100 percent on college. I couldn't concentrate and finally faced the reality of my life. I had to return home to mother, Morris, and manufacturing. Morris and I were full partners again when, in June of 1947 after that school year, I returned to the business. It would be years before I lost my embarrassment at not finishing college.

Back in Medway, I was working 18 hours a day and carving out a business that would take shape into something bigger than I ever dreamed about in that damn soggy foxhole outside of Aachen. Looking back on 1947, I realize that my decision to leave school and get back into business with Morris was the right decision for me.

Little did I know that the next year I would make the best decision of my entire life.

CHAPTER XVI

That Glorious Feeling

You've heard me talk a lot about my brother Morris, but it was my younger brother, Joe, who helped make me a very happy man. Joe and I have never been close, then or today, but I had nothing better to do one night and Joe talked me into going to a party with him. He said there would be a lot of girls there, but he had said that before and I had never gone.

She was shy and quiet with an air of sincerity. Her name was Janet, but I began calling her Jan from the start. I felt more comfortable with her than with any girl I had ever been around. She reminded me of my mother. She was good-looking and well-dressed, but a lot of girls are good-looking and well-dressed and don't have that certain something I saw and felt when I was with her.

A lot of guys say this, but with me it was true. I knew right from the beginning that this was it. This was the girl. This was the woman I wanted to marry.

"Can I take you home?"

"Well, you can take me to my truck."

"Take you to your truck? What are you talking about?"

"I left my truck at Virginia's house and I would appreciate your taking me there."

I thought this cute little girl was kidding me, but I took her to her girlfriend's house and she got into this little dry cleaner's truck and drove out of my life for that night. However, I did have her phone number, which I thought meant I would talk with her soon. I was wrong.

I called and called and called, and the only person I ever got was her father—we became telephone friends after a couple of weeks. Finally I found out she was going to night school and I needed to call at a different time. When I did, I finally got to talk with her, but that was equally as frustrating because she claimed to be too busy to date.

What a struggle I went through, but she finally agreed to a date. We went out and had a wonderful time. I was more convinced than ever that this was the girl I wanted to marry. I have been a salesman all my life, and I never wanted to close a sale as bad as I did this one, but I could see that this was going to be tough.

In the first place, she wasn't the kind of girl who was going to rush into anything as serious as marriage without being very sure I was right for her. Second, she was the kind of daughter who had a mind of her own, but her mother was against Jan seeing me.

Jan's father was a great guy, but her mother was a snob. To the mother, I was a peddler son of a sweat shop tailor, while Jan's father was a fine tailor with a dry cleaning shop of his own. She had great ambitions for her daughter, and they didn't include Charlie Nirenberg.

Happily, while my family was low class to Jan's mother, my mother and Jan got along great. When I saw Jan and my mother together, I realized even more what a wonderful, wonderful person Jan was and wanted to marry her right then. But I took it slowly and carefully.

Many people think of me as a serious-minded, no-nonsense business type, but I enjoy having fun and making fun just as I did on that night after Yom Kippur. Jan had just spent the holiday with us. We got into my ice cream truck and went to a dimly-lit cocktail lounge for a drink. Since she had just met my family, she was a bit nervous as to how they had received her.

She had given me her high school ring as a symbol of our friendship. As we sat in the semi-darkness, I took it off.

"This is it. I'm giving you back your ring."

Her eyes got big as I took her hand and slipped a ring on her finger. She was on the verge of crying as she looked down at her hand, "This isn't my ring!'

"It isn't? Well, I'll be darned."

Of course, I had palmed the high school ring and slipped a diamond engagement ring on her finger as my way of proposing to her. She left it on her finger and cried as her way of saying "Yes." In my heart I knew I had made the smartest move of my life. I never had any doubts about her being the one and I still have no doubts today.

I couldn't say that about her mother. She was not a happy woman when she found out about the engagement, but there was no going back because Jan had made up her mind. Even so, just because she had to endure her daughter getting married to a lowlife peddler didn't mean she had to like it. So she refused to give Jan a big wedding. Probably figured we would get a divorce soon, so why invest too much money? We were married on January 26, 1949—just a day short of three years after I got out of the service.

There were twenty members of my family at the wedding, but only five of hers. We understood that was another way of showing displeasure with the match. It hurt me deeply, but I didn't want to say anything about it. It hurt me because I was proud of what I had achieved and I loved my family and was proud of them—particularly my mother whose struggles had made this possible.

Beyond that, it seemed like a mean-spirited, small-minded thing for Jan's mother to do. She hurt her daughter because of me. That's what pained me the most. The woman I loved was being hurt by someone against whom I had no defense.

To underscore the point, when Jan's sister got married some years later, Jan's mother invited 300 guests. Our modest wedding was a way of letting us know that she was not real thrilled about her daughter marrying me.

One thing I knew. I was not going to live in an environment where the two women I loved most in my life, my mother and my wife, were going to be constantly insulted because of our marriage. I talked it over with Jan and we decided to move to Springfield, some distance away from her mother, which would relieve us of day-to-day reminders of her.

We made our plans before we married, including talking to Morris about expanding our business. I told him he could stay in Medway and take care of the business we already had, and I would go to Springfield and develop new business. That was fine with him.

The month before we married, we went to Springfield and found an apartment so it would be ready. But we didn't have a car. When we dated, we always used one of my peddler trucks, but I had worked long and hard enough and thought we deserved a real automobile.

Coleman Finklestein was a Chevrolet dealer and a friend, so I called him and asked him to sell me a new car for my honeymoon. Production of new automobiles had halted during the war, but the new 1949s were just coming out and I wanted one.

"I can't give you one until mid-February, Charlie."

"Why not, Coleman? I know you already have them."

"I know, but the Chevrolet people will skin me alive if I let any of them out of the garage before mid-February."

The conversation seesawed between me telling him how badly I needed the car and him telling me how he couldn't give it to me. I finally wore him down, and he agreed to sell me one if I would take it in the dark and not let anyone see it until I left town after our wedding to drive to Florida on our honeymoon.

It sounded like a good deal, so I picked it up at night and put it in a garage until our wedding day. Then off we went to Florida in the new car the day after we got married. That's when the trouble started. We didn't get very far before a cop pulled us over.

"What did I do, officer?"

"Nothing, young man, but I just have to see this new Chevrolet you are driving."

So the trooper and his partner started looking it over. I was so proud I opened the hood and the trunk for their inspection as if I were a car salesman.

At the first stop light, it was the same thing. People crossing the street had to look inside, and I could hardly go because of the mob swarming around the car. I didn't open the hood or the trunk this time, because we had other things on our minds and other things we wanted to be doing.

It was a slow trip to Florida, because we were stopped over and over again by policemen. When we came out of our motel room each morning, a gang of curious onlookers was gathered around the car looking and asking questions.

The truth, of course, was that I was so proud of my new wife and my new car that I could hardly believe I was just little Charlie Nirenberg, an ice cream peddler from Millis—now Springfield—Massachusetts.

Shortly before we married, I told Jan, "Look, I want you to know that you are not marrying a flunky. You are marrying a guy who is going to become a millionaire someday."

She smiled and said, "Gee, that would be nice. I'm glad you think that way."

She didn't laugh or put me down. She had faith that I would make it. More than that, I understood that my becoming a millionaire was not the important issue. What was important was that I loved her and she loved me and we would be together and support each other no matter whether I was a millionaire or a pauper. That, as it turned out, was put to the test years later.

I found the woman I loved, and I wanted her with all my heart. In spite of the obstacles put in my way, I persisted, I endured, I refused to give up. I finally married her and am still married to her 43 years later!

CHAPTER XVII

A New Life and a New Business

A LOT OF important things happened the year I met and courted Jan, including some changes between Morris and me.

First of all, it was a big move for Jan and me to go to Springfield, because it was a lot bigger than Millis and I had to get our operation there started from scratch.

I couldn't afford an office, but I needed a base of operations where I could distribute ice cream from my large truck to the peddlers and their smaller trucks. Later, I planned on establishing commercial accounts with stores in the area to supply them, but in the beginning I wanted to go the easy route—the route that I knew best, peddling.

There were lots of service men and women coming home and looking for a quick job, and I had one for them. They would buy an ice cream truck from me and I would set them up with a neighborhood route, supply them with the ice cream, and teach them how to sell. More important than having a job, they had an immediate business of their own.

I soon had a crew of peddlers lined up ready and eager to start, but I still lacked a base of operations.

There was a service station at 1025 State Street with a large lot in the back that I thought could be my base. I met and talked with the owner, Pop Coviello.

"Pop, you need gas business and I need a place to operate. You have a back lot you're not using. I want to park my wholesale ice cream truck back there and plug the refrigeration unit into your outlet.

"Then a whole slew of peddlers with small trucks will come by and load up ice cream. They are going to spend the day cruising neighborhoods and when they come back, they'll need gas. They'll buy from you and you'll do one helluva lot of gasoline business."

Pop was counting the money he was going to make on gas in his head, but he was a cool customer and he didn't give me a yes or a no. He just stood there thinking and looking at me.

"Pop, I am not going to let you lose any money on this deal. You show me the highest electric bill you've paid in the last year. If you have one any higher after I start plugging my truck in, I'll pay the difference"—big sport that I was after getting his place rent free.

He said one word and that sealed the deal.

"Okay."

What I said to Pop has always been a principle of mine in business. The only kind of business deal that makes sense to me is one that makes sense to everyone in the deal. The only good business deal is a deal where everybody profits. Anyhow, Pop and I had a deal that we would both profit from having.

So I got on the phone that night and called all my peddlers, and we were in business. I couldn't make them buy their gas from Pop, but most of them did, and it turned out to be a good deal for everybody.

The next morning the truck from Medway came. I plugged it in and parked my car next to it. My car became my office. As peddlers showed up, I wrote up their orders for what they needed that day. The peddlers paid me in cash in advance and I stuck it in a sack under the front seat of the "office."

Jan was with me, and we both loaded up the peddlers' trucks. That first year we loaded ten trucks a day.

Things were going along beautifully, capped off by the arrival in September of our first daughter, Sandra Lee, whom we have always called Sandi.

What a great year for an ex-Red Ball Express driver and

platoon sergeant. The peddlers made money. My brother and I made money. Pop was making money. My wife made a baby. I was walking on air.

Then my brother shot me back down to earth!

It happened in the fall of 1949, during what's supposed to be the quiet season for the ice cream business, but turned out to be firecracker hot for me.

We were back in Millis to spend the winter so that we could visit with relatives and show off the new baby. Morris and I spent time planning and talking about some unfinished business.

Three years earlier we had gotten involved with the "Kenro Vendor." We wanted to develop a vending machine that dispensed chocolate-covered ice cream bars. A machine dispensing ice cream in a Dixie Cup was already on the market, but nothing that delivered a chocolate-covered bar. Then we found a Philadelphia company that had what we wanted. Morris and I went to see the two principals, Jim Kendrick and Sam Rogove.

What a sight we must have been to these two city hustlers. We walked in and there was this huge, foot-long cigar in the office with Sam Rogove attached to it. With him was the smooth-talking, polished fashion plate Jim Kendrick. We were all supposed to be in the ice cream business, but it turned out those two were in the dry cleaning business and they took these two country boys to the cleaners.

"Look, if you give us $3,000 now, we will give you the entire New England region as exclusive distributors. The Kenro Vendor is going to be on the market within six months. We'll give you the first six machines off the assembly line as part of the deal and, since they will sell for $500 each, you'll have all your money back plus the New England region."

"Naturally, we'll give you an override on every machine that is sold in your territory. This is your chance to get in on the ground floor."

Hey, we went for it. Only now, three years later, we hadn't seen a machine or heard a word from our dear Philadelphia friends. What we had seen was some of the Kenro Venders and we had seen them in our territory.

We hired an attorney, Abe Handverger, who claimed he

couldn't make progress, so Morris and I decided I should go down to Philadelphia and check out the situation. A few days later I was there, in the office of the gruff attorney with whom our attorney was supposed to be dealing.

"I'm Charlie Nirenberg from Golden Meadow Ice Cream, Medway, Massachusetts."

"Whadda ya want?"

"We bought the exclusive rights to New England for the Kenro Vender and we're seeing competitors using the machines in our territory, besides never getting the machines we bought for $3,000. Our attorney Handverger says you won't even answer his letters."

"Never heard of your deal and never heard of your Handverger."

I knew good and well it would do no good to see the two con men who had taken our $3,000. It would have been a waste of time, and I wasn't in the mood to watch those two clowns laugh in my face. I had to do something else to save what I could of this deal.

"Let me ask you this. Since you know nothing about this, would you be interested in being my attorney and getting back our $3,000?"

"All right, I'll represent you, but it's going to cost you 25 percent."

I quickly figured that $750 to him left us with $2,250 and was better than nothing. I agreed to the deal.

The next day I was back in Millis walking into Morris' office feeling pretty cocky about myself. There was a chance now that we could get $2,250 which was better than losing the whole $3,000. My cockiness lasted about 14 seconds after I explained the deal to Morris.

Just like the time I first got run out of the sewer pipe factory, I expected sympathy and praise, but that wasn't what I got. Morris blew his stack.

"Who in the hell gave you the right to give them 25 percent without checking with me?"

Rocked back by the ferocity of his outburst, I gulped and said, "Morris, you agreed that I should go down and try to get our money back. I did the best I could. I am a partner in this

A New Life and a New Business 113

company. THAT gives me the right to make the deal without checking with you."

[By the way, we did collect the $2,250 within 60 days.]

I'm not sure he heard what I said, he was so mad. Smoke was coming out of his ears and I was afraid he might have a stroke, because he went on and on. I know I didn't hear most of what he said. I wondered if he was under pressure from his illness, but that probably wasn't it, because he had done this as long as I had known him.

I finally left the office, hurt and disgusted all at the same time. The next day we met again.

"Charlie, I'll get right to the point. We're not getting along. Either you buy me out or I'll buy you out."

"You know I can't buy you out. I had to get a G.I. loan to even put $4,000 into this company. How can I buy you out?"

"All right, I'll buy you out."

The successful Nirenberg & Nirenberg venture was dissolved. He ended up with the Golden Meadow Ice Cream Company. I got two notes totaling $15,000, a $5,000 refrigerator truck now and a second used truck in a year, plus $1,100 in cash to cover eleven weeks' salary. For a $4,000 investment, I was coming out with about $25,000 in assets, but only $1,100 in cash.

After working night and day to build the business, I basically had in hand a refrigerator truck and $1,100 cash, along with a wife and new baby.

Still, I came out ahead in at least three ways. First, I was forced back on my own with the experience and contacts to succeed, and that's how I have always operated best—as my own boss. Unfortunately, there would be times when I would forget that and would suffer for it.

Second, Morris and I became better friends because we were really better at being brothers than we were at being business partners.

Finally, I was the mover and the shaker, and alone I could go much faster. After I left, Golden Meadow pretty much stood still. By contrast, the company I formed grew and is still growing today.

Through all of this upheaval, the two women in my life—

actually, there was now a third, but she was only one year old —stood by me, advised me, and gave me the strength to be who I am. My brother Morris set me free, and the women in my life gave me strength.

CHAPTER XVIII

Another New Beginning

SOCRATES SAID THAT every man should marry. If he gets a good wife, it is the greatest gift the gods can bestow. If he gets a bad wife, he can become a philosopher.

Well, I never became a philosopher because I have a wonderful wife, which was demonstrated again when I came home from the buyout meeting with Morris and told Jan what had happened.

"I may be digging ditches, but I am going to find out if I can do it on my own."

"For whatever it is worth, I am with you all the way." Well, I'll tell you what it's worth to have a wife who has faith in you. It was worth the million dollars I told her I was going to make some day. She gave me the great gift of faith over and over again during our marriage. She hasn't always agreed with everything I've done and that's a good thing. But over the years, she has always had faith in me.

Faith can make a man. Lack of faith can break him.

Her faith was critical at the time, because I had mixed emotions and uncertainties that day Morris and I parted company. I was sad because we had worked together for so long, and I was glad because I was now free to do what I wanted to do. I knew it would be tough going for awhile, but I was confident and enthused.

These are the important ingredients in starting a new business: *confidence* and *enthusiasm* shored up with the *faith* of someone you *love*. Without these things you start out with fear and doubt and the chances of success are slim.

I spent the next 24 hours thinking and planning, and when I came home Jan was reading the classified ads looking for a job.

"Put the paper down, honey. Let me tell you how we're going to do it."

She looked and listened as I explained how I had worked things out in my mind. "I am going to the bank with one of the notes Morris gave me and borrow money against it."

The next morning I was sitting at the desk of Alexander Gufanti, a banker at the Springfield National Bank known for giving potential borrowers about three minutes of his time. He gave me ten and seemed genuinely interested in my business plan. I didn't have experience dealing with bankers—Morris did that—and I was lucky to connect with this kind of understanding banker.

"Come back in a week and I'll let you know."

A week? That was a disappointment. My brain was spinning with my plans and I was enthused about getting started NOW. Also, I wanted to come home to Jan with a victory to justify her faith. But I had to wait a week before I could return to Gufanti's desk again with hope in my heart and a smile on my face.

"Charles, I looked at the material you gave and I'm impressed. The bank will discount the note for you."

So I put up one of Morris' notes for $5,000. The bank immediately deducted its interest and gave me the balance. It was now late January, and I had two months until ice cream season started when I founded the Country Club Ice Cream Company.

What I needed was ten more ice cream peddlers who would buy from me, just like I had organized the first ten the year before working out of Pop's back lot. So, I plunged in and took a gamble. I ordered ten ice cream trucks for $2,200 each, or a total of $22,000, when all I had in the bank was $4,000, and began advertising them for sale to peddlers at $2,500 each.

The money from the first buyers, of course, had to be used to pay for the trucks before I could take delivery. It turned out there were a lot of people with $2,500 who wanted to be their own boss. By April 1st, I had sold all ten trucks and had this additional fleet to service with ice cream out of my large refrigerated truck. Morris and I had split in late January. Two months later I was in business with one major difference. I was the boss—the only boss—and that was something I liked.

My first year of 1950 on my own went fine. By the end of September, the season was over, and I had nothing to do until April 1st of the next year.

My routine was to get up in the morning, go out to buy the newspaper, have a little breakfast, read, and do the crossword puzzle. This demanding schedule occupied me until 10 o'clock, at which time I could then turn my attention to telling my wife how to do the housework.

She was raising Sandi, keeping books for the company, cooking the meals and everything else, but, for some silly reason, I seemed to think she didn't know how to dust.

"Hey, you missed a spot on the coffee table."

"A little more to the left on that shelf."

Predictably this only went on for a couple of weeks, until one morning, when I was giving her the benefit of my superior wisdom about dusting, she blew her top.

"Charlie, you're driving me crazy. Get out of this house and don't come back until dinner time the way other husbands do!"

Naturally, she was right. I was being a jerk, but only because I was bored and needed something to do. At least, I THINK that was why I was acting like a jerk.

Then, as it has many times before in my life, the light bulb went in my head. I had ice cream trucks that were idle from September to April. Why not convert one into a canteen truck? Please understand that making more money was not the primary object. I just had to find something to keep me busy. It's my nature and, since Jan had thrown me out of the house during the day and I sure wasn't going to work for someone else, I decided to sell coffee and donuts.

In a way, I was learning another important business lesson that would be the subject of case studies at major business schools, except that I learned it in practice and, at the time, I didn't even realize I was learning it.

The classic case used in business schools at Harvard, Wharton, and Stanford is the failure of the railroads to get into the then-profitable airline business in the 1940s and later. The reason is that railroad people thought of themselves as being in the railroad business. In fact, they were in the *transportation* business, and the train was only the current mechanism.

By the same token, I had thought of myself as being in the ice cream business. In fact, I was in the convenience food business. People bought ice cream from our trucks because it was convenient and saved them time.

So I went downtown and purchased the largest thermos jug I could find from Kittredge Equipment. I think it held ten gallons. Then I found a coffee pot that made ten gallons of coffee and an insulated chest that would seal up donuts and keep them clean and fresh. It was out of season for ice cream, but I was in business again.

Each morning I got up at 6 o'clock, brewed a ten-gallon batch of coffee on the stove, and filled up the thermos. I stopped at a local bakery to pick up fresh donuts and drove out to construction sites around Springfield.

Men [they were all men in those days] working on construction sites didn't have time to go a couple miles to get a coffee and donut on their work breaks, so I brought the coffee and donuts to them. And if I charged them a little more, so what? They were willing to pay extra for the convenience—for the time-saving. There would be a message in that for me later in my career.

There was one glitch in my operation. It was named Miss Mason, the landlady who lived on the first floor of our apartment building. One morning Miss Mason stopped me.

"Mr. Nirenberg, your coffee sure smells good every morning."

I laughed.

"I do like my coffee strong, Miss Mason."

She would have kicked us out if she knew I was brewing coffee commercially in the apartment. Miss Mason was an old maid right out of Central Casting in Hollywood—very prim and proper with pince nez glasses, polite but stern with dresses touching the floor and buttoned up to her chin. She looked as if she never missed a meal, but maybe she missed a lot of other things in her life.

She also would have kicked us out if she knew how I was able to keep our apartment heated. Here we were with a baby in this old building with windows so loose you could feel the wind blowing when you were six feet from the window.

She had a heating system with a lock on the thermostat that was set at 68 degrees. If the windows had been caulked, it might have been bearable. But when I checked the temperature six feet from the window in the living room, it was 40 degrees. Something had to be done.

I checked the thermostat lock and there was no way to change the setting without breaking the lock. I thought a bit and then it came to me. I put a few ice cubes in a glass on top of the thermostat. The temperature went down and the heater kicked in so we finally got some warmth.

Suddenly, I heard someone coming up the stairs. I figured it was Miss Mason and took the glass off and put it in the refrigerator. When I opened the door, Miss Mason was standing there looking stern.

"The thermostat seems to be stuck, Mr. Nirenberg, maybe I better check it."

She carefully inspected the thermostat.

"Does it seem rather hot in here for you?"

"No, it seems rather comfortable to me."

Ignoring what I said, she unlocked the thermostat and turned the setting down two degrees. Then, she left and I put the glass of ice back on the thermostat.

We played this game all winter, but she never caught on to what I was doing. I was careful not to overdo it by getting our apartment too hot, which was impossible anyhow, but I got it warm enough to be liveable.

Meanwhile, things were expanding in my new convenience food business.

The fact that I was in the convenience food business was brought home when my regular customers asked for sandwiches in addition to coffee and donuts. I soon learned that construction workers ate like there was no tomorrow. Naturally, I turned to Jan.

"They keep asking for sandwiches. Do you think you could make a few before I leave each morning?"

She did, but soon a few became a lot. Still, Jan never complained. She is not a complainer and, besides, it was probably worth it to be spared my advice on dusting techniques. Still, when I converted another truck and hired someone to work for me as I expanded the canteen routes, I was getting some dirty looks. That decided me that I should take Jan and Sandi to Florida for a couple of weeks of sunshine at Christmas time.

While we were gone, I hired two peddlers to cover the canteen routes with the two trucks. When I came back, I just kept them on the payroll. I spent my time converting more trucks and expanding the routes, until I had ten canteen trucks on the road every morning.

The second year I was in business on my own, I sold 25 trucks at $300 profit each, and was making money servicing each of them with ice cream. That year, 1951, I made $10,000 clear in the ice cream season alone, which was more than a lot of doctors and lawyers were making working all year long.

On top of that, the canteen business was going well and I would stick with it for another five years. That all came about because my wife kicked me out of the house.

There is a serious message here, but I don't know what it is, except that not everybody has a wife willing to kick her husband out of the house and let him end up being a workaholic.

CHAPTER XIX

A Double Test of My Will

Good as times were at the moment, there were some rough waters right ahead of me that would test my will. Testing my will may have been good or it may have been bad, but it certainly was unpleasant.

The most unpleasant test was another conflict with Morris. We were not business partners anymore, but still DID business together, in that I bought my ice cream from what was now entirely his plant at Medway. I set up a separate company, but I was using the same ice cream, except that it was turning out not to be the same ice cream.

By midsummer, customers were complaining to my peddlers that the ice cream wasn't as good as it had been. One of the things I knew intuitively was that people are very fussy about what they eat. You can't fool them with a substandard food product and, once you lose their loyalty by selling them a bad food product, they'll never come back to you. You are tainted about to something that is very important to them.

So, when the complaints came to me, I took them very seriously and investigated immediately. I found, to my dismay, that my brother was doing what we in the business call "putting the bicycle pump" to the ice cream. He faced profit problems and solved them by pumping too much air into the ice cream. When I sold boxes of chocolate-covered ice cream bars to the drivers, they came back and said, "Charlie, the ice cream was so light, it just blew away!"

I struggled with this situation through that summer and discussed it gingerly with Morris. He was family and he was sick physically, but I was family, too, and this could make me sick financially. Morris wouldn't change, so I had to change. Incidentally, although the doctors told Morris he only had a little time left to live, he continued to live for more than another 30 years.

The next year, I bought my ice cream from the Sealtest Ice Cream Company, which had a plant in Springfield that was more convenient for me anyhow. I hated to do that to my brother, but he didn't hate to do it to me, so what alternative did I have? In any case, I now had a better product to give my peddlers and soon had a lot more peddlers, too.

Always expansion-minded, I moved into the Hartford, Connecticut, market down the highway from Springfield and soon had 20 trucks working that area. During the third year on my own, 1952, I put another 20 peddlers in Pittsfield, Massachusetts, giving me a total of 65 trucks a day I was servicing with ice cream.

From that day three years before when I found Jan reading the classified ads to find a job to support us, we had grown to 65 ice cream trucks, plus ten canteen trucks and a good sized commercial ice cream business that sold wholesale to small stores year around.

1952 was a curious year elsewhere, with the King of England, George VI, dying and being succeeded by his daughter, Elizabeth II; and, Dwight D. Eisenhower—my old Army buddy —being elected President.

Casting about for new horizons, I started selling to the larger markets. That's when my will was tested for the second time in the same year. Sealtest had its own sales force calling on stores of all sizes, but I used to bootleg a few items and outsell them.

I made a very good deal at a rock-bottom price with Sealtest, because I was buying for all my 65 trucks. As a result I could sell some selected Sealtest products to stores for less than the Sealtest salesmen could. Well, that couldn't last for too long, and it didn't.

One day the Sealtest people called me in and said, "Charlie, you can't sell any more Sealtest ice cream to our store customers. We have our own sales force that will handle that."

"Well, that's entirely up to you. If you want me to buy my ice cream from someone else, I will."

No, Sealtest didn't want that at all, and its ultimatum was softened to more of a warning. I got the message, but this test of wills was also a case of the handwriting being on the wall for me. These people were going to restrict my business to conform to what was best for them and not what was best for me. That rubbed me the wrong way. Besides, I was doing better than I had hoped when I started in 1949. Most important, I had to keep growing, because Jan was also growing with a new baby on the way.

It was winter time and I didn't have that much to do, so I decided I had to build my own ice cream plant. By February of 1952, I had built a new building with a room for making ice cream and a freezer storage room for keeping it. We also had a new son, Larry. So February of 1952 was a month of creation and new additions. It all made Jan and me very happy people.

By the time the ice cream peddling season started, Sealtest had cut me off, but I was already in production with Snow White Princess Ice Cream which was made the way I wanted ice cream to be made—namely, the richest, creamiest, best ice cream on the market. It soon was a best seller in the region.

Here is a story about somebody starting in business and making a new product, ice cream, namely, Snow White Princess Ice Cream. He has very little money, but needs marketing to promote a product that has to compete with Sealtest, Hood's, Borden's, and other national names, so he has to be a little bit creative.

Let me tell you how my marketing program developed an interest in Snow White Princess Ice Cream.

I had to figure out something that wouldn't cost me millions of dollars. I did invest what was an awful lot of money to me to promote a product—$5,000. Let me tell you, that was an awful lot of money to me at that stage.

Here's what I did: other people were running beauty contests with beautiful girls who were 17, 18, 19, and 20 maximum—mostly teens. Beautiful girls showing up in bathing suits.

I thought about it and said, "Nobody is running a beauty contest for little girls." So I had a Princess of the Year Contest in 1956. The way you entered the contest was, you went to the store and bought a pint of Princess Ice Cream, then sent the cover in, along with a picture of your little girl who was anywhere from two to 12 years old.

The panel of judges was elected officials, newscasters, and others who would select from those pictures. We had a room full of pictures, and it was difficult to select the finalists, but they got it down to 40 or 50 finalists.

Next, we took half an hour of television time, and out of those 40 or 50 finalists we selected the Princess of the Year and five runner-ups. Her picture was in the newspaper and in all our stores. Secondly, we took her and her family to dinner and, thirdly, she won a brand new bicycle.

I think we got more publicity out of that campaign for $5000 than people can do today for $100,000—maybe even $200,000. It was one of the most successful marketing campaigns that I believe I have ever run.

The mayor of Springfield was there, and I still have people talking to me about that contest. Just the other day I had somebody come in to see me whose daughter was the first runner-up to the Princess of the Year.

I realized quality always has a place in the market. This philosophy carries to Dairy Mart today, and our stores are known for giving the customer top-quality service and top-quality products. We could cut corners, but we won't. It doesn't pay. Morris never learned that and, while he stayed in business, he never grew.

My confidence in Snow White Princess led me to use a taste test that would later be used by a soft drink company. I used to go into the big super markets with a container of Snow White Princess Ice Cream and pitch the buyer. He almost always responded, "Well, you know we carry Sealtest ice cream and have for the past 25 years."

"You carried it for 25 years? Don't you think it is time to at least consider a change? Taste my Snow White Princess Ice

Cream, and if you don't think it is better than Sealtest, you'll never see me in here again."

I put some Sealtest in one paper cup and Snow White Princess in another while they turned their backs. They had an assistant watching so I didn't pull any tricks.

Then I handed them the two cups, and said, "Taste whichever you care to first and then the other and tell me which you like the best."

Snow White Princess won nine out of ten times, and by the late 1950s we were selling Snow White Princess to several hundred stores.

Selling store by store took time and a lot of work, but I always did it myself whenever we had a new product or were trying to break into a new market.

Too many businessmen try becoming executives too fast when they start a company. My style was to stay out in the field and learn the products and the market. I never felt the need to play big shot. Even today I go out into the field and make surprise visits to our Dairy Mart Stores. I want to know, face to face, how we can help our managers and franchisees, and you can't do that by memo or from behind a desk.

Also, you can't keep tabs on what's happening in the market place and what customers want by relying on reports, newsletters, memos, and messengers. You have to be there. You have to sense it and experience it.

> *Charlie built Dairy Mart himself and has done practically every job in the place [unlike the MBA types who run companies these days].*
>
> *"Anybody in this company can look around and realize that whatever job they're doing, the chairman probably did at one point."*
>
> *Importance of morale is a central Dairy Mart doctrine, "It's one of my major philosophies of life! I tell all our people, you've got to enjoy your work! And if they don't enjoy their work, I ask them to please find another job."*
>
> —University of Massachusetts Magazine Profile, Winter, 1992

In the mid to late 1950s, America was sensing and experiencing a lot of things—some of them exciting and some of them disturbing.

One of the most exciting was the nationwide explosion of television, particularly after the completion of the cross-country coaxial cable that made national television a reality. When we got our first little black-and-white set, I never fantasized that someday I would be the star of my own Dairy Mart TV commercials, with strangers recognizing me on the street and asking for autographs.

In 1963, I was 40 years old, married to a wonderful wife, with a mother I cherished and three healthy children, plus I had made a significant success of my business. No one in the world was standing taller than Charlie Nirenberg.

CHAPTER XX

America and Convenience Stores in 50s

AMERICAN LIFE CONTINUED to change in the 1950s and for me, things were going great. They got even greater when my wife introduced me to our third child on July 31, 1955, a darling girl we named Pamela Jean.

President Eisenhower appointed Charles E. Wilson, the president of General Motors, as Secretary of Defense. A colorful, controversial character suffering from foot-in-mouth disease, Wilson said things like, "What's good for General Motors is good for America." What caught my attention was his rebuttal to his critics saying, "I didn't come down here to run a grocery store."

That may have been his problem. If he had understood how to run a grocery store, he would have understood more about dealing with people. Meanwhile in Springfield, Massachusetts, I was a Charlie who HAD come to run a kind of grocery store called a convenience store.

The convenience store concept had been developed by the Southland Corporation, which was now expanding its chain of 7-Elevens.

In the same vein, I was always looking for new ways to build and expand my convenience food business, and I was attracted to the convenience store idea. I was supplying several convenience stores, and I noticed that other suppliers of dairy products, bakery goods and the rest came into the stores and set up their wares, often providing equipment including shelves and signs, while the store operator did little. That looked interesting to me.

Frozen TV dinners had become the rage. The several million women who had entered the labor market during World War II stayed and were joined by several million more. They didn't have time to a bake cakes from scratch, so Betty Crocker put the cake premixed in a box and they just had to stir and bake. Swanson put roast beef, mashed potatoes, and green peas on an aluminum tray and froze it for later reheating.

America became—and still is—a nation in a rush, dedicated to making every minute count. Convenience and saving time is what it's all about, and that's what Dairy Mart is still all about today.

The supermarket had grown popular, but that was for big shopping. On the way home from work, people who didn't want to take the time and bother of going to the supermarket would stop at the convenience store for a loaf of bread, a gallon of milk, or a dozen eggs.

By this time, after Pam was born, I had over 250 accounts for my wholesale ice cream business. We were making a comfortable living, but I could see it would be a long, long time before I would make the million dollars I promised Jan. This is when my sixth sense of business told me I could do it quicker by getting into the convenience store business.

Actually, I wasn't "getting into that business." I was already in the convenience food business and had been for several years. I was just taking the wheels off it and giving it a permanent location.

In 1957, when I found an empty grocery store in south Springfield that had gone out of business, I saw my first chance. I took over the store and stocked it with four kinds of items: milk, ice cream, eggs, and bakery products. Outside I put up a sign calling it Dairy Land.

That was the first mistake I became aware of, because soon a letter came from an attorney saying his client delivered milk under that name. My lawyer and I talked and decided it wasn't worth fighting about, and I called the sign painter.

Standing outside looking at the Dairy Land sign, my mind was working to see if there was anything I could salvage of it. Signs cost a lot of money, and I couldn't afford to waste any when I was starting a new business. Then in my mind's eye I saw that I could have a new name by just changing three letters. If I hadn't heard from the milkman's lawyer, today there would 1200 Dairy Land stores instead of 1200 Dairy Mart stores.

At the time I got into the convenience store business, there were only 500 such stores in the entire country, with about 200 of them being 7-Eleven stores owned by the Southland Company. So, while we weren't the first, we were among the pioneers in the industry that has some 80,000 stores today.

The Dairy Land name was the first mistake I became aware of in this new venture. However, it wasn't the first mistake I made. Looking back, I should have known that if the grocer before me had gone out of business, why would I succeed in the same location in a similar business? The answer is that I wasn't that smart at that time.

I later learned that *location* can be everything in the convenience store business. In fact, real estate brokers have an old saying that the three most important factors in buying real estate are location, location, and, of course, location.

So, the sign was fixed and we were off, but hardly running. In fact, barely crawling says it more accurately.

What I didn't understand was that there were a lot of apartment houses around this location and that meant a lot of people, which should have meant a lot of business. It didn't. I began to wonder why the guy before me hadn't made it. In time, I found out.

There were a lot of apartment houses and a lot of people, but they were mostly older couples instead of young couples with growing families. Older couples don't buy much milk, while young couples buy lots of milk.

What I had failed to do was to stop and think about the customers. Who were they? What did they want? I thought about that when I was vending ice cream in neighborhoods and factories and running canteen trucks to construction workers. But for some reason I didn't apply that same street smart logic to my first convenience store.

In time, I would find out that all of this has a fancy name in the business schools. They call it demographic research and analysis. I had never heard of "demographics," which is what advertising people build campaigns around. As a result, my first store was the worst store I ever opened! A complete failure!

At that point, if I had really been smart, I would have given it up. I would have folded my tent, gone home, and forgotten about the convenience store business. Instead, I kept that store going for a year and didn't close it until after I found a good location and opened my second store. It was in an area loaded with young couples, with lots of babies and kids growing up.

This store was a success from day one. So what had I done? I learned from my experience and didn't repeat my past mistake. And I refused to give up! Persistence—determination—had paid off again.

Things looked good, but one of the worst things that would ever happen to me in business was only months away.

CHAPTER XXI

Banker as Bastard

I STILL HAD to cope with the problems of a wholesale ice cream business, and it was time to visit my friendly banker. My friend Alexander Gufanti had retired and had been replaced by a man by the name of Collin Cathrew. Still, I was a good customer and had always repaid my notes with the bank as promised and I was armed with a decent financial statement. It was mid-October and the business through September, the end of the ice cream season, showed I had had a good year. I explained to him that in the past I had borrowed $10,000 in December each year to take care of the rebates I owed my accounts at that time. This was one of the big selling points with these accounts. The more of my ice cream they sold during the year, the larger their rebate would be in December. It was like a Christmas bonus to them.

We visited a while and Cathrew looked over my statement and approved the loan on the spot. I said, "That's great. I appreciate it, but I don't need the money right now. I will come back in December and sign the note."

So when December came around, my efficient little wife, mother, and bookkeeper made out the rebate checks. I told her to go ahead and mail them, and I would go by the bank the next day and sign the note so they could put the money to cover the checks in my account.

After all, my friendly new banker had told me that I could have the money. Lesson number one in dealing with a banker: take the money when they offer it to you. Friendly or not, bankers can be strange business partners.

I was all dressed up and all smiles and all ready to get my $10,000 when I walked into the bank the next morning. Mr. Cathrew smiled as we shook hands and then said: "You have to see Fred LaPage about the loan you have requested." I was a bit stunned, to say the least, as my understanding was that I already had been approved for the loan, but only replied with, "Why?"

His head hung just a tad as he said, "I can't talk about it. All I can tell you is that Mr. LaPage, our senior vice president in charge of the commercial loan department, wants to talk to you."

The Springfield National Bank of that day was a big, impressive, marble building with high ceilings and walled partitions around desks on the floor where officers could talk to customers. These walls were more like dividers, because they were only about four feet high, topped with glass about two feet high. This gave the impression of an office, but without any ceiling except the one another twenty feet or so above the desk. It afforded very little privacy and it was not too difficult to hear the conversation going on at the next desk.

It was the first time I had ever seen Mr. LaPage, and he got right down to business with:

"I've got bad news for you, Mr. Nirenberg."

"What do you mean?" was my question.

"We're not going to be able to give you the money," was his answer.

I could not believe my ears and spit out, "You what?"

"I think you heard me, Mr. Nirenberg. We are not going to give you the money you requested."

"Hey, it was more than a request," came out of the rather deflated Mr. Nirenberg. "I was promised that money by your Mr. Cathrew."

"I have the final say on all loans, Mr. Nirenberg, and I find you have a covenant on your Small Business Administration loan that says you cannot expand more than $30,000 in any one year. You expanded $33,000 on new capital equipment last year," came from this not-too-friendly banker.

"So?" was my response.

"So, you have violated the covenant, Mr. Nirenberg, and your note is now a current liability and due and payable in full." His words hit me like a freight train.

I said, "But the Small Business Administration has not said a word to me about this. They must not be worried or complaining."

Mr. LaPage looked at me like he was enjoying his job and said, "I know, but I am. You are not liquid in my opinion, and therefore I am not giving you the money."

At that, I stood up and said, as loud as my best sergeant voice could, "YOU SON OF A BITCH!"

All work stopped, and it seemed that every eye in the bank was on Mr. LaPage and Mr. Nirenberg. With that I turned around and walked out and vowed to myself: there will come a day Mr. LaPage, there will come a day. And it did come, but it did take a while.

When I walked in the door, Jan took one look and knew I had not gotten the loan. I was so mad I could hardly talk, but she calmed me in a hurry with, "Now, Charlie, I don't know what happened at the bank, but getting your blood pressure up is not going to help one bit. We have been in tough spots before and found a way out of them. Just forget the bank. If we talk about it, I know you will find another source for the money you need."

She was right, of course, and once more I must emphasize the value of having a mate who believes in you and stands by you, but I was really in a predicament. I had checks in the mail to all of my customers, and the checks were no good. They would soon be bouncing all over western Massachusetts and northwestern Connecticut. I had never given anyone a bad check in my life, and now, all of a sudden, I had almost 250 bad checks on the way to people I considered friends. The embarrassment of one hot check would have been bad enough. How could I explain my problem or face all of the people who had been buying ice cream from me for years?

Jan and I went over the books and the bank statements and

outstanding checks and any assets we could possibly sell to see where we stood and how much we would need as a minimum. When it was all over, we could come up with $4,000, so we still needed $6,000. That was not quite as bad as needing $10,000, but my eyes were watering. It was such a helpless feeling—a feeling I imagine most people who have started a new business experience before the business is finally on firm ground.

I was so sick to my stomach that I could hardly think straight. Then Jan said, "I know the interest rate will probably be two or three times what the banks are charging, but why don't you try Household Finance or Beneficial Loan? You have a good credit rating and have always repaid your notes. Why don't you see if they will let you have $6,000?"

I looked both ways to see if there was anybody I knew watching as I stood in front of the Household Finance office in downtown Springfield. I would rather have been charging that German pillbox again than opening that door.

But open it I did, and who should I end up facing but a young man who knew me. His name was Mike Corvin. I was so embarrassed I could hardly talk. It would have been much easier talking to someone who did not know me, but I did manage to tell him I needed $6,000 and I needed it soon!

Mike's reply was at least encouraging: "Call me at home tonight. I may be able to help you, Charlie." I went home with my head held just a little bit higher, but I tried not to get my hopes too high. I was still smarting from the way the bank had pulled the rug out from under me. Pride is a great asset, but sometimes, too much pride can be a detriment. Looking back, I think I had too much pride that day and had taken my setback at the bank on too much of a personal basis.

When I called Mike that night, my spirits went up another notch when he said, "Meet me at Bob Draymore's office tomorrow morning at 10 o'clock. I think we may be able to help you, Charlie."

I did not sleep well that night, but I at least slept better than I would have if I had not gone to see Mike Corvin.

Bob Draymore was an attorney in downtown Springfield. I knew of him, but did not really know him. Bob became a very good friend. I will never forget what he did for me that day.

I have always believed in honesty, so I laid it all on the table. I told them of my problem with the bank and my problem of having hot checks in the mail. Businessmen don't normally go to Household or Beneficial for business loans, so I felt I should level with them. Bob and Mike laughed and said they had heard stories similar to mine before.

Then they said I could have the money I needed and that they had a standard interest rate of 18 percent. The bank was going to charge me six percent, but they might just as well have said one percent since they were not going to give it to me anyway. So I had no problem with 18 percent. I could not let my customers down. The note with my new-found friends was due on August 1 of the next year. This would give me plenty of time, because by August the ice cream business would have been booming for a couple of months.

I never did know who had loaned me the money. My guess is that it was Bob Draymore, because I later found out that he occasionally made loans, so it was probably him. Perhaps Mike had taken me to him because of the size of the loan. It does not seem like much today, but in 1960, $6,000 may have been over the limit for Household. Either way, I am indebted to both Bob and Mike and still consider both of them friends today.

Strange how things work out. Years later, Mike Corvin came to me needing financial help and I was truly happy to be able to extend a hand very much in the way he had helped me. I have always remembered my friends who helped me get started in this business. I always wonder about the successful man who says that he did it all by himself. I have found so many nice people along the way who have helped me and I honestly don't think that I would be where I am today without their help. This most certainly includes bankers. There are many fine bankers who dedicate their lives to helping young people get started in the business world.

Bob Draymore and I became good friends and, sadly, the last thing I was able to do for him in this life was to help bury him a few months ago. I was recuperating from an operation over the Fourth of July when the depressing news came that Bob had died on Sunday, July 5th. I really wasn't feeling that good, but I would never let Bob leave us without being there to wish him Godspeed.

He had been there for me 32 years ago and there was no way I wasn't going to be there at the end to tell him "Thank You" one more time.

CHAPTER XXII

A Tale of Two Problems

IN THE LATE 50s and early 60s a lot of things happened in the world that would have long-term effects on all of our lives, even Jan's and mine.

My deep involvement was in events that would have a long term effect on the future of my business and my family. At this time, it focused on two incidents and two men, Irving and Joe.

The first was a run-in with Irving Feinstein, who ran Grower's Outlet stores, which was one of my oldest and best wholesale ice cream customers buying about 25 percent of my output. One day, Irving called me on the phone.

"Charlie, do I hear correctly that you own the Dairy Mart stores?"

It was a temptation to lie to him, because I knew what was coming next, but that's not my style.

"That's right, Irving."

"Well, you're going to have to decide, Charlie. You are either in the retail business or the wholesale business."

Now, understand that Irving could take the skin off of your back without you feeling it. He was a wonderful man, but also a shrewd businessman who was the best buyer I ever met. He knew how to buy right, and in business that's just as important as knowing how to sell right. One of the reasons I loved talking with him is I always learned something.

When I started doing business with him, one of the things I learned was that he was a slow pay and liked to work on my money. He did the same with other suppliers and really allowed his suppliers to float his business. He was using their money.

I would deliver ice cream and give him three months to pay. He always took an extra 15 days beyond that and, of course, he had already gotten his money from selling the ice cream I had delivered three and a half months before. We call this working the float, and Irving was a master at it.

Hey, I didn't like the arrangement, but I did like Irving's business and one came with the other. Besides, Irving was a nice guy.

So, back to the day he said I had to choose retail or wholesale. This was one of those times I figured he was bluffing me.

"Irving, I suppose you're right. I guess I have to make a decision. But let me say this first. I don't see my four little convenience stores being any competition to your big chain of supermarkets. I am just small potatoes compared with you."

Here I was using one of Irving's own techniques I had learned. Namely, set up the other guy with flattery just before you move in for the kill.

"But I have to be honest with you, my friend, I built those four little stores the hard way and they're doing pretty well for me and I plan on expanding them."

"Oh, really?" he jumped in.

"Yeah, really. But if I double them or even triple them, I am still not going to hurt you. You are a decent guy, Irving. I have learned from you and I admire you and I will miss doing business with you.

"On the other hand, I am giving you good ice cream at a price lower than I am giving anyone else. So I hope you won't worry about my insignificant convenience stores because I want to continue our mutually beneficial business relationship for many years to come."

"Just testing you, Charlie, just testing you," he said, after ten seconds dead silence while he digested what I had said.

"Now tell me the truth, Charlie, am I really getting ice cream at a lower price than anyone else?"

"Yes, you sure are."

Irving laughed a laugh of satisfaction.

"Just forget I called, Charlie, just forget I called."

When I hung up, I laughed, too, because I had called Irving's bluff and skinned him for a change! But I didn't forget that he called. His call in fact made me turn over in my mind my business arrangement with Irving and analyze just how good it was.

I don't know what I would have done that day if he had called my bluff, but I do know what I did that day because he did call. As I looked at it carefully, I really wasn't making a lot of money from the Growers Outlet account. If he had called my bluff, I might have chosen my convenience stores over his ice cream business anyhow.

Because Irving was a slow pay who at times owed me up to $100,000, and because I couldn't sit around waiting for my money, I had to factor his debt to me. That is, I had to go to a bank and factor it, getting only 80 percent up front. When the check came in three months later, I got the other 20 percent.

Still, this is something a person has to do at times when starting a business on a shoe string. It takes years to grow, and growing takes more and more money, so it becomes a vicious cycle. Growth was what I had to have to reach that goal of being a millionaire, and cash flow is what it took. It was, as the proverb says, like riding a tiger: you don't want to stay on, but if you get off, you'll be eaten. Irving Feinstein was one tiger, and Joe Langdon was the other.

Irving's call made me do some serious thinking. The difficulty of getting enough cash to expand and grow also made me do some serious thinking. That's how I got involved for a time with slick Joe Langdon.

In order to survive and succeed as an independent businessman, you sometimes have to do things you don't feel comfortable doing. I wasn't comfortable walking into Household Finance to try to borrow the $6,000 I needed, but it worked out. I also gained two good friends who actually lent me the money. I wasn't comfortable with the possibility of losing Irving's business, but keeping it meant factoring his accounts at high interest rates.

When Joe Langdon came to see me, I admired his daring—that always was a weakness of mine—but I really wasn't very comfortable with the guy. Even so . . .

Anyhow, there he was in my office giving me his pitch about how I should hire him to sell Dairy Mart franchises and that would get me the capital to grow.

"I want to show you how to sell franchises. I hear you are trying to grow, and I'll show you how to do it."

"What do you know about selling franchises?" I asked, because he had hit upon a nerve—I did want to grow.

Then he took off with a nonstop talk, going on for ten minutes about what a great salesman he was. Significantly, he didn't say anything about selling franchises or much of anything else. I stopped him.

"I'm going to tell you something. I can see you don't know a damn thing about franchising, and you know even less about convenience stores."

He was taken aback and stared at me like a deer caught in your headlights who was certain it was about to be run over by a semi truck.

"But you have a hell of a lot of guts, and I like a salesman with guts. When do you want to start?"

That caught him flat-footed surprised.

"Really?"

"Yeah."

"I'm ready to start right now."

"Okay, Joe, I am opening my seventh store soon. Why don't you go franchise that store? Find someone who wants to get into the business who has some money and we've got the store for him."

I sold my franchises for $5,000, which barely covered the cost of merchandise and equipment, but figured I would make my profit by selling the store ice cream. Joe didn't agree with that.

"Hell, Charlie, let's get $8,000."

I still didn't know if Joe was all hot air, but $8,000 sounded good, and there was only one way to find out if he could get that much.

"Do you really think you can get $8,000?"

"Yeah! We can get $8,000, Charlie. You pay me $1,000 and you get the $7,000."

"You've got a deal, Joe."

Who would have thought that some day I would be getting $100,000, $150,000, and even $200,000 for a Dairy Mart franchise?

Hot air or no hot air, I liked the guy's nerve. I gave him the papers for our Dickinson Street store #7 and let him loose. I didn't realize that, instead of letting Joe loose, I should have let Joe go. The warning signal came a week later when he reappeared in my office.

"I've sold Dickinson Street five times."

"What do you mean five times?"

"I have five different people who want that store. They have the money and they're ready to sign the papers."

"You can't sell the same store to five different people. What in the world is wrong with you, Joe?"

"Well, what am I going to do, Charlie? These people want to join your organization, so I just kept selling them."

"Joe, pick the best one and tell the other four that Dickinson Street was gone by the time you got to see me, but we'll be opening other stores every few weeks and they can have one of those. You line 'em up, Joe, and I'll open 'em up."

That's what he did. Man, he was a smooth operator. I didn't know it then, but the first day he came in to see me for a job, he already had a bunch of leads in his pocket from a blind ad he'd been running in the classifieds. He was so sure he could make a deal with me, he ran the ad before meeting me and without telling me.

I gave him a desk in an office over the ice cream plant and soon saw a lot of people going up and down the stairs. I'm a man who has to know what's going on all the time so I approached Joe.

"You sure have a lot of candidates for stores coming, Joe."

"Oh, no, I'm interviewing for franchise salesmen."

"But, Joe, I can't build the stores as fast as you can sell them, much less what more salesmen would sell, and I can't pay both you and someone else a commission."

"No problem, Charlie, I'm paying them $500 out of my $1,000."

"What do you mean 'them', Joe? How many salesman are we talking about? How am I going to find the locations and put the packages together that fast?"

Joe laughed. "Hey, you wanted to grow, didn't you, Charlie?"

He was right. I realized that this is the way companies were built, but it still left me uneasy, even though some of the people he hired, like Bob Comstock, were dynamite salesmen. Maybe too dynamite. Dynamite can blow things up.

Joe and Bob convinced me they should go to Hartford and sell franchises in that area, even though I had only been opening stores in Massachusetts up until then. That sounded fine to me. I knew Hartford, since I had previously run ice cream peddler trucks in that area.

As I said, I have to know what's going on—that's just the way I am—because I don't like uncertainty. And I was still queasy about Joe and the way he thought. So I went to Hartford unannounced to check out how he and Bob were selling franchises for my company. Naturally, I was very sensitive about that, because it was MY company and MY reputation that was on the line. It's the same thing that drove me to cover those rebate checks.

These two guys convinced me that they should get a hotel room and do the franchising in Hartford, but when I had not heard from them for a few days, I decided that maybe I should go over and take a look to see how things were going. I didn't call in advance, just stopped by the desk of the hotel and told the clerk I was there to see Mr. Comstock. He said, "Oh, yes," and gave me his suite number. He was very cordial and it was obvious that he knew Mr. Comstock well. I later found out that these guys had rented the suite by the week, had the furniture moved out, and a desk put in, and really went all out including paying the clerk off so any prospects coming by would be properly impressed.

When I got off the elevator, I could see that the door had been left open a few inches so it looked more like an office instead of a bedroom. It was also so Bob Comstock could hear anybody getting off the elevator.

Naturally, he did not know it was me, so by the time I got to the partially opened door I could hear him saying, "Now, I told you, Mr. Johnson, we screen our candidates for a franchise very carefully, and you simply have not met our standards." I opened the door, but Comstock paid no attention to me. He continued on the telephone with, "I told you all of this before, Mr. Johnson. I know you have the money, Mr. Johnson. No, no, no, you can't pay me extra. I am sorry, Mr. Johnson." Then he put the phone back on the cradle and looked up to find me standing there. We both started to laugh.

As far as he knew up until that point, I was another prospect he was trying to impress. The prospects would hear him turning down some guy over the phone, but to the guy who came in the door he would end up saying, "You know, I have plenty of people who want a piece of this action, Mr. Smith, but we turn them down if they are not the right person for our operation. But after talking to you, I can just look at you and see you are the right guy for the store we have coming up."

I sat there and watched this guy in action with a prospect. When the prospect said he wanted the store, but had not brought his checkbook, he would actually say, "I tell you what. Do you have $100 on you? Give me the $100, and I will hold this store for you until you can go get a check and come back within the next hour with $900 more for the down payment. That is how much I think of you. I just know you are the man I am looking for and this is just the beginning of a long and mutually profitable business relationship, so I am going to do this for you."

At that point, I realized I had two con men working for me. They were smooth. They were slick. And I started to worry and watch them more closely. In just a few weeks, Bob Comstock had sold and gotten checks for ten new stores, and I brought their operation to a halt. As it turned out, I had to end up giving five of the checks back. I simply could not deliver suitable stores, stores in the right locations that would make both of us some money, as fast as these guys could sell them.

This is a good example of how I got an education in the franchising business when we really started to grow. We have a franchising department today, but I assure you that we do not operate that way. In fact, we don't even franchise a store until it has been in operation for at least a year. By that time, we know pretty well what the store will do, and, frankly, we also know what it is worth.

I went on to open another 33 stores in the next ten years and could have grown as fast as Joe wanted, but I was cautious. I not only wanted the right location, I wanted the right standards of operation. I wanted the BEST stores. I wanted stores that were clean, with help that was friendly. I wanted good stores and good people.

I wanted stores that were stocked with the right amounts and the right merchandise. This is an art with the convenience store, because of the limited space the store has and the limited time the customer has.

Today we have computers that tell us what the people want and what moves off the shelves in a hurry. In the beginning for us and for other pioneers in the convenience store industry, it was a SCIENCE called "guesswork."

Joe Langdon later sued me, claiming I had promised him 25 percent of the company. This was just about the time I had become a paper millionaire through sale of the company to Giant stores, which you'll read about in a coming chapter.

I insisted on fighting the case, even though my lawyers said it would have been simpler to settle and avoid the expense and nuisance. The very reason that I let Joe go was the very reason I decided to fight. I had to do the right thing, the honest thing for myself, if not for anyone else.

It took several years to get to court by which time I was a paper pauper, but the jury still thought I was this rich businessman mistreating this poor old Joe, and it awarded him $20,000. I spent that much again in legal fees. I could have settled earlier for $5,000, but this was a matter of principle.

A year later, I ran into Joe at a convention.

"Well, Joe, who are you taking today?"

He grinned sheepishly and kept on walking.

I learned another lesson because of my friend Irving. Growers Outlet had become Jumbo Food Stores, and then Big Y Supermarkets bought out Jumbo.

They did not give me so much as the courtesy of using all the ice cream I was holding for them with the Jumbo label in my freezer. I kept half a room filled with Jumbo ice cream so I could deliver promptly whenever they needed it. I had to sell it at a big discount just to get it out the door. So we lost that account. And we lost money because of the way Big Y treated us when they took over.

I was pretty shook up for about 30 days while all of this was happening, and then I realized that Big Y had probably done me the biggest favor of my life. I was now going to have the $100,000 that I had been using to finance that account available to expand my controlled outlet business.

Selling on a very slim margin can be tempting because of the volume involved, but it can also be risky because of unforeseen events. Bottom line, I would have always been at the mercy of the large customers who are continually squeezing their suppliers because of competition for the shopper's dollar.

When I finally analyzed it that way, the truth hit me. Big Y had done me a favor. They really had not hurt me that much, but if I had kept them as a customer under the same terms I had had with Irving, it could have caught up with me eventually and caused me to go broke.

They forced me to look into different ways to make a profit from the ice cream I was making. That is exactly what I did, and the different way became the Princess Ice Cream Parlours.

CHAPTER XXIII

The Princess Ice Cream Parlours

I WAS ALREADY making an excellent ice cream that I was selling through wholesale outlets and my own convenience stores, so I thought, why not sell it directly through my own ice cream parlours?

Sometimes one gets so busy and so involved with basic business he doesn't have time to back off and look at what he is doing—or not doing. I have been guilty of that, and so are a lot of other business people. We lose our perspective. As the man said, when you're up to your ass in alligators, you sometimes forget your original objective was to drain the swamp.

The ice cream parlour of that day was not very exciting. Friendly Ice Cream was the big gun in the field, and their shops were dull and stagnant. There is something special about ice cream. I remember the Ice Cream Look I first recognized when I started out selling ice cream bars in the sewer pipe factory. The thought, the concept, the mood of ice cream is that of anticipated pleasure.

I wanted something different from the Friendly approach. Something that created the mood of ice cream. Something with charm and still some pizzazz. Something the customers would tell their friends about, building word-of-mouth clientele. Something that would be as different from the Friendly approach as Disneyland was from the weekend ferris wheel in the supermarket parking lot. It was that approach that I liked.

For starters, Princess Ice Cream Parlour was the perfect name. I was already making and selling Snow White Ice Cream, and everybody knew Snow White was a princess even though she hung out with Seven Strange Little Men. So that was the name and the easy part.

Then I remembered that ice cream was basically a six-months-of-the-year product. How could I make my Princess Ice Cream Parlours a year-round operation? Another lesson came to me from my convenience food experience of the past several years. Just as I learned when I converted my summertime only ice cream trucks into year-round canteen trucks, I would offer other things to the consumer besides delicious Snow White Ice Cream.

Maybe I should include sandwiches, but why limit it to sandwiches? People like to go out for breakfast and dinner, when they don't just want sandwiches like they do at lunchtime. So why not a restaurant? Still call it Princess Ice Cream Parlour, but offer a restaurant menu to broaden the customer base. That's what I did when I went from a coffee-and-donut canteen truck to a sandwiches-and-snacks canteen truck. It was amazing how the lessons of the past provided a light for new business in the future.

Next the mood and physical arrangement started to form in my mind: Tiffany lamps above each booth would add class; and flocked red velvet wallpaper would give it a warm, turn-of-the-century look. Before long, I had what I wanted: a beautiful and different ice cream parlour that was also a restaurant for customers year round.

By 1972, I was proud that I had created five Princess Ice Cream Parlours. There was a gentleman by the name of Walter Andrews who was running the Princess Ice Cream Parlours.

Walter Andrews was a gentlemen in the true sense of the word. He had taste and style, and he ran the Princess Ice Cream Parlours for me. He knew antiques and was the guy who really put the final package together and made the parlours stylish. He did an outstanding job decorating and managing all five parlours.

In the expansion of any business, finding the right people to manage the business is important. You need someone who will run your business as if it was their own. Walter was that kind of man.

So, it was 1972, I had 37 convenience stores, a profitable wholesale ice cream business, and five restaurants. Life was good, and I was convinced I was on my way to making that million dollars I had promised Jan years before.

CHAPTER XXIV

In Heaven Enroute to Hell

IT STARTED INNOCENTLY enough with a conversation between two men—one of whom I knew and one of whom I had not yet met.

"You know, I love those Princess Ice Cream Parlours. I would like to buy them. Do you know the guy who owns them?"

That was David Harper, an Englishman imported by Giant Stores to run its snack shops, talking to my friend, George Kittredge, who ran an equipment company I had dealt with over the years.

"Sure, I know him well. He's a good customer and a friend. Want me to call him for you?"

The next thing I knew, David and I were lunching. Just listening to his British accent impressed me. Near the end of our meal, David made his point.

"Charlie, I like you. I think you should meet the chairman of Giant Stores."

"What do I need to meet him for?"

"Well, I'm not certain, but I believe he might be interested in purchasing your company."

That struck me as funny, but it did answer my curiosity about why he had invited me to lunch in the first place.

"David, I really don't think that I have any interest in selling right now. Things are going well, and for the first time in my life, I can relax and enjoy life."

Like any good salesman, David took the turndown cheerfully and made sure to keep the door open.

"Okay, but let's keep in touch."

Naturally, I wasn't going to tell David everything that was going on because it wasn't any of his business. Moreover, it had to be kept confidential for the moment.

I didn't tell David that I was about to go public with my company; that is, sell shares of stock in the company for the first time. We had good growth, but, always pushing ahead, I wanted SPECTACULAR growth, and going public seemed the way to raise the money it would take.

By 1972, when I opened my fifth Princess Ice Cream Parlour, we were doing $2 million a year in gross sales for the combined businesses, and the bottom line—the net profit after taxes—was $72,000. I realized I was a long way from being a millionaire, but going public would shorten the journey.

This was my chance to get the company in position to take advantage of the CHAIN BELT OF OPPORTUNITY when it came rolling by.

In September, 1970, I started to get things ready for my next move. I went to Arthur Schatz, a Hartford lawyer, and told him of my dreams for Dairy Mart. Up until then, it was touch and go to show a profit each year because I was pouring everything I could back into expanding the business. Sometimes I poured back too much.

I was only taking a meager $11,000 a year in salary. Even so, the company only showed $20,000 in net profit. I wanted to move on, to expand and get the benefits of size, but I couldn't generate enough cash to move fast enough.

Schatz listen to my story and then brought in an associate who had recently joined the firm, Stanford Goldman, into the meeting.

"Now, Mr. Nirenberg, I want you to tell Mr. Goldman the same story you have just told me."

So I told of my dreams of the future again, perhaps embellishing it more than the first time because I felt good chemistry between Goldman and me. He was 27 and I was 46, and neither of us had forgotten the power of a man's dreams. Yet, he knew the practical side of what had to be done if I was to raise money by going public.

"Mr. Nirenberg, if you're going public, we cannot use these accounting figures. You have to use an accounting firm people will believe—one of the big names in the field."

I had always used the same accountant my brother and I had when we were partners. He produced simple, easy-to-understand statements that were all I needed. However, I understood what Goldman meant. When you are dealing with other people's money, confidence and image are important. I had learned that many times over in my business, where I did all I could to maintain the confidence of my customers and to keep a good public image. So we brought in Bob Adams, the head of the small business department of Arthur Andersen & Co.

Then began months of frustration, because my "books" consisted of bales of loose papers stuck in various drawers and filing cabinets. It was an accountant's nightmare, and the first Arthur Andersen man, John Latetze, gave up. Then Adams brought in another man, Larry Handler.

Now things began to fall into place, and Larry was pushing ahead as hard as he could. I suppose I sometimes put too much importance on small, symbolic things in my judgement of people, but it has generally served me well. In this case, I was impressed that Larry gave up Thanksgiving dinner with his family in order to finish up my financial statements.

By early December, Larry had come up with an impressive financial statement that pleased me and Bob Adams.

"It looks like we have something to show them, Charlie."

It was a professional job of the specialized kind you need to show potential investors, giving both the past and the future of the company. Stanford Goldman, who I now called Ford, liked the statement, and we went ahead with the public filing of a modest $500,000 stock offering.

I would be giving up part of my company, but I would be getting the money I needed to make it a much bigger company.

We officially filed the papers for the stock offering on December 31, 1971. The phone call came two days later, and I wish I had never answered it.

"Charlie, this is Ted Kaufman, Chairman of Giant Stores. David Harper may have mentioned me to you."

"Yes, we had lunch and he . . ."

"Charlie, David told me about you and your wonderful company and the Princess Ice Cream Parlours."

"Well, Mr. Kaufman, we talked about them."

"Ted, please, Charlie. Call me Ted.'

"Okay, Ted."

"Charlie, I like what David told me about you and your company and we've talked it over here at Giant. As they say in the movies, Charlie, I am going to make you an offer you can't refuse. I am going to make you a rich man, Charlie, a very rich man."

"I don't know, Mr. Kaufman, er, Ted . . ."

"Give me just a moment to outline what I'm talking about here. You've got a great little operation, but you need capital to expand and make it really sing.

"That's tough when you are a small independent, but if you were part of the Giant family, you'd be part of a dynamic, growing company that made $600,000 in after-tax profits in 1969, $900,000 after tax in 1970, and $1,300,000 after tax this last year."

Kaufman was trying to impress me. And, funny thing about it, he did. Even so, I had an obligation to some people who had worked hard to take my company public in a hurry.

"Mr. Kaufman, I just . . ."

"Ted, Charlie, please."

"Ted, I just filed a Reg A issue to raise $500,000 to expand my stores. I'm really not sure this is a good time for us to talk. If you'd called earlier, I might have jumped at the chance to be associated with your fine company, but this isn't the right time."

Ted Kaufman didn't have a lot of people say no to him and he wasn't about to give in. So he pushed me some more.

"Charlie, don't worry about the stock issue. We'll take care of all the expenses that you've had putting it together."

Well, I admit that caught my attention. This man was a dealmaker. All he wanted to know was what it took to make a deal and he was ready to move. It was interesting to observe it, except I was doing more than just observing it, I was part of the deal he was making.

"We're talking of somewhere between $50,000 and $60,000, Ted."

"Is that all, Charlie? No problem. No problem at all. Now please come over and see me. I want to show you our operation. I want you to meet some of my key people.

"You know, Charlie, we're already strong in the discount store business and we're moving into catalog showrooms in a big way. Now we want to get into convenience stores and restaurants. As a part of us, what you have started at Dairy Mart can soon become a giant in that field, too."

Of course, it is always nice to be wanted and appreciated, and my new friend, Ted, made me feel that way. It sounded as if he really wanted me and my stores, and he did. I drove over to Chelmsford to meet Ted and was treated like visiting royalty. Another lesson I was forgetting at the moment. That was the way the tiger, Irving, always treated me just before he skinned me.

Oh, Giant was a big operation, and these were big people. They were listed on the American Stock Exchange. I was in the big time. This was the big league. I was a kid who had just fallen off the pumpkin truck to them, and they knew just how to manipulate me. It is hard for a proud man to say that, but I am realist enough to know what happened.

The deal they crafted was marvelous in its detail and sounded like the fulfillment of the dream of this little ice cream peddler who started selling chocolate-covered ice cream bars to roughnecks in a sewer pipe factory.

I would get 43,000 shares of Giant Stores stock the day we closed the deal, plus another 43,000 shares over the next five years.

All the expenses of my aborted stock offering—about $60,000—would be paid by Giant. And Giant would put up $500,000 for Dairy Mart to expand.

I would remain as President of Dairy Mart and become a vice-president of Giant Stores under a five-year contract paying me $40,000 a year. Big money in 1972 and a lot more than the $20,000 I was now paying myself.

Wow!

And the stock? When we started negotiating, Giant Stores

stock was selling at $18 a share. By the time we closed the deal, it was up to $26 a share. I would be worth $2,236,000.

In the few days it took to work out these details, my new friend, Ted, had my full attention. Giant Stores looked good. Ted looked good. The deal looked good.

"How many suits can I wear, Charlie? How many ties? I don't care about the money. It's the challenge. I'm proud of what we've done here at Giant, but it's only the beginning. We're going places, Charlie, and we want you to be part of our success."

The "we" was Ted, President Jack J. Shapiro, Financial Vice President Benjamin Leiberman, and Treasurer Gerald Silverstein, who were all in the room with me.

When I walked into that conference room, my feet sank into the plush carpeting up to my ankles. When I walked out of that conference room, my feet were a foot above the carpeting.

That was January 9th, just one week after the first phone call from my new friend, Ted. The next day, I went back to talk with my old friends, Bob Adams and Ford Goldman. I felt I had to discuss the deal with them before I agreed to anything.

We talked, we discussed, we analyzed, and we weighed both sides of the deal. Then Bob concluded, "This looks like a great deal for you. Your company had a profit of $72,000 after taxes this last year and we can't be sure the public will buy the stock in the offering that would give you the $500,000 you want.

"On the other hand, Kaufman is offering you Giant stock worth around two million PLUS the $500,000 for expansion PLUS the $60,000 you sank into the stock offering PLUS he assures you a free hand in running Dairy Mart.

"For the life of me, I don't see how you can walk away from this one, Charlie."

I couldn't see how I could walk away from it either, and one month later we sat in Giant's corporate headquarters and signed all the papers.

I went home that day and gleefully said to Jan, "Remember the boy who told you he was going to be a millionaire someday? How does nearly two-and-a-quarter million sound to you?"

Naturally, she was thrilled, because she, too, had put thousands of hours of hope and some hours of tears into our company. We had made it to the top side by side.

It was a wonderful day, and both of us knew we wanted to share it with my mother, who was then living at the nursing home. This meant a lot to Jan and me, but to my mother it was a miracle beyond her wildest dreams. The heart-wrenching struggles, humiliations, and dangers she had survived to make it to this day must have flooded through her memory when Jan and I told her of our success, the family's success—of her success.

Her determination and native guile had brought us to this time. And her incredible self-reliance.

I don't believe there was ever a day that I was happier than the day I could prove my worth and the worth of my dreams to the two women upon whom I built my life: my wife and my mother.

My mother died six weeks later, and it saddened me at the time. Later, I was grateful she had died and didn't see what happened to us in the year that followed.

CHAPTER XXV

The Devil in a Double-Breasted Suit

THINGS SHOULD HAVE started moving faster and faster for me with the backing of this big company, and I worried I might not be able to handle all the work. I shouldn't have worried.

It felt good to be part of the Giant organization, which, at the time, had over 40 discount department stores like the K-Mart chain. They had just opened two catalog-showroom stores and were negotiating to buy 10 more. It was a company doing $100 million a year in sales and growing like mad. I was a lucky man to be part of it.

My timing was perfect, because the convenience store industry, led by the Southland people, was exploding. They were expanding like crazy and we needed to do the same thing—not so much by building new stores, but by buying up existing chains.

In short, there were a lot of opportunities for Dairy Mart to blossom into a major chain. With the backing of Giant, I felt we were on the threshold of something big.

They took the management of the Princess Ice Cream Parlours from me and gave them to David Harper, who had first gotten me into this operation, but I didn't mind. I figured it gave me more time to run Dairy Mart.

One of the kicks of being associated with Giant Stores was

that at least once a week there would be a glowing report on the company in a trade journal or the business section of a newspaper. It had become the darling of Wall Street stock analysts.

May 30th was a big day for me, when the company gave me a lunch in Boston with all their main people on hand and, more importantly, gave me my 43,000 shares of stock.

During lunch, I chatted with Ted.

"You know, Ted, I should have asked for some cash with our deal. I never took much money out of Dairy Mart. As fast as I made some, I opened another store. I used all my cash for growth."

"No problem, Charlie. All you have to do is take those shares we just gave you to the First National Bank of Boston and they'll let you have 75 percent of the market value."

"Really?"

"Sure, just tell them how much you want and they'll tell you how much stock you have to put up. They'll put the money in your account or give you cash. Whatever way you want it."

That was a big day in my life. I was welcomed into the Giant company, they said nice things about me at lunch, and that afternoon I had $200,000 deposited into my bank account. Money in my pocket, money in my bank, and half a million dollars to spend making Dairy Mart grow.

I began to think about expansion when I heard about a chain of convenience stores in Rhode Island that might be for sale. I went to work on it, checked out the chain, and went through channels at Giant. I talked with the people at headquarters until finally I had a very good deal worked out for buying the entire chain of 60 stores to add to our 37.

I worked out an impressive purchase proposal and sent it into the home office. July passed and nothing. August passed and still nothing. September came and the stores went—to someone else—Leon Cornell had bought the chain. I was fit to be tied.

I had followed all the procedures of the company and didn't get a word back. Not an okay. Not a go-to-hell. Nothing.

I picked up the telephone and called the President, Jack Shapiro,

"What did you do to me? I worked up a good deal to move

into Rhode Island in a big way. I had everything ready to go and you guys held up approval so long, I lost the deal. What the hell is going on?"

Well, for the next ten minutes he talked like a politician—a lot of words, but no meaning. He reassured me of his faith in me and that I was going to go far with Giant and hung up.

That's the way it went from then on. Even to open a new store, there would be delays and footdragging. When I found a location where we could have a store and pump gas, I got enthusiastic. This was something new in the convenience store business back in 1972, and I was high on the concept.

I called Giant and was told to work up proposals and projections plus an artist's rendering and send it to this guy and that guy. This wasn't the way I operated. When I found something and had a hunch, I moved and I moved fast. But there was no moving Giant. I hung up the phone, discouraged. It was like the guy who tried to modernize the bureaucracy at General Motors who likened it to trying to teach elephants to dance.

Even so, I was trying to be a good Giant executive and I followed their silly instructions to the letter and sent off the package of material to the proper people.

Months passed and I didn't hear a single word from headquarters. Then the same thing happened as with the Rhode Island deal—somebody else got the location. This was getting to be like a bad movie that I saw over and over again—except I was starring in this one!

Then I finally heard from headquarters. It was an invitation for Jan and me to join the other executives of Giant Stores and their spouses for a two-day get-together at a fancy hotel. It was nice. At $100,000 for the 100 of us, it should have been. Lots of socializing and small talk until the final banquet, when the top guns grandiosely announced they were spending $2 million to advertise their new catalog showroom stores.

It was quite a show they put on for us that night, but it didn't erase a thought in my head that I foolishly shared with some of the other executives.

"Gosh, I never heard of anyone spending $2 million advertising an operation that wasn't doing more than $10 million in sales. Seems like a very large advertising budget."

Naturally, they laughed out loud, but thought to themselves,

"What does this yokel farmer from Springfield know about big business and catalog stores?"

When we left that Sunday afternoon, I was disillusioned, and alarm bells were going off in my Springfield farmer head telling me there was trouble here. It was bad enough that I couldn't get any deals through the Black Hole in Space they called headquarters. I now realized that these people were lousy businessmen. They weren't realistic, and they didn't know what they were doing.

Worse than that, my future and the future of the stores I had worked so hard to create was in their hands!

The next day, I dispatched a letter to Ted and asked to appear before the Giant Stores Board of Directors. That wasn't received well, and after some hemming and hawing, I was finally allowed to appear before the Executive Committee made up of Ted's hand-picked cronies.

I spoke for about a half an hour and told them that I had a little company out in Springfield where 12 people were doing the work of 24 and it seemed to me that Giant was a company of 2,400 people doing the work of 1,200. And, as a stockholder, I was not thrilled about that.

It was November, 1972, and I had only been on board with Giant since February. Ted scowled at me, "What are you worried about, your stock?" His tone was unnecessarily sarcastic.

"You bet your ass I am worried about my stock!"

My tone was necessarily sarcastic.

Nothing happened then or in the next three months except for an occasional phone call. My honeymoon with Giant was over, and I was outnumbered and outvoted. I was also out of sorts, because I knew I was right and hoped I was wrong. I was very nervous about the future of Giant.

I became particularly nervous about the Financial Vice-President, Lieberman, who seemed to come up with glowing bottom-line figures much too fast. Ted had projected record earnings for fiscal 1973, and his source of information was Lieberman, who was too slick for me.

Normally, Jan and I take a two-week or so vacation in Jamaica every February, and this year was the same. I really needed to get away this time. The stress of uncertainty with Giant was troubling me.

I was right to be troubled, because when I returned to my Springfield office, I immediately sensed something was wrong with my people. They were obviously down about something and avoided looking me in the eye.

"What's going on? What's wrong with you people?"

"Haven't you heard, Charlie?"

"Haven't I heard WHAT?"

"Giant Stores is going to file for bankruptcy!"

The words slammed into me like somebody had hit me across the chest with a two by four. It almost drove me to my knees. I went into my office gripped by a chill and called Shapiro. It was the same baloney.

"Don't worry, Charlie, everything is going to be all right. We're having a few problems, but the banks will bail us out."

Don't worry? You're damn right I would worry, because I felt this son of a bitch wasn't leveling with me again. I had trouble believing what he told me. He had misled me so many times he now insulted my intelligence by thinking he could do it to me again. It got to the point that, if I saw Shapiro's lips moving, I couldn't be sure if he was telling the truth.

Helplessly, I watched my paper fortune evaporate. It sold at $26 a share the day our deal closed. Now, nine months later, it was down to $20. Soon, it slid to $15, then $12, then $10, then $8, then $5. Picking up the newspaper every morning and turning to the financial page was like opening a vein wider and wider as my fortune bled away. Then, it was going for $3, then $2, then $1, and, then they filed for Chapter 11 and it was zero. Absolute zero.

I was almost 50 years old and had worked hard for at least 40 years. Ten months ago, I was worth $2,236,000. Now I not only had nothing, I owed the bank $200,000! Thank God my mother wasn't alive to see it.

CHAPTER XXVI

A Victim of Liars and Crooks

I THINK I was right about Jack Shapiro. I don't believe that son of a bitch would know the truth if he saw it.

Two weeks after Shapiro told me everything was going to be fine, I was totally wiped out. During that time, the First National Bank of Boston called me fourteen times saying I had to put up more Giant Stores stock to cover my $200,000 loan. It finally had all my stock—all 43,000 shares. It was worthless, but just to keep their bookkeeping straight, they wanted more of it to cover my loan.

That wasn't the only example of stupidity. The next major example was the bankruptcy court appointing a guy from Tandy Stores to come in and save Giant Stores. If this guy had been the captain on the Titanic, his solution to saving the ship would have been to rearrange the deck furniture.

Here came this big, tall Texan with a ten-gallon hat loaded with more hot air than Kaufman and Shapiro combined, and that's a load. The first thing he did was throw Ted out of his job and his office. Shapiro, Ted's loyal-to-the-death right hand man, helped carry Ted's desk outside, locked the office, and told Ted to hit the road. What loyalty! Ted promptly lost 100 pounds in 30 days from the stress.

A dramatic move, but what Giant needed at that moment was solid businessmen, not drama coaches.

Shapiro was now in charge, but reported to Charles Tandy every time he had a thought, itch, or need to go to the bathroom. Tandy's own key people were really in control.

Meanwhile, I called every day. My line was different every day.

"I want to talk with Tandy."

"You guys stole my company."

"I want my company back."

The objective was the same. I wanted to talk with Charles Tandy in Texas. Finally, I got him on the phone and pushed him into having a meeting with me at Giant headquarters in Chelmsford.

Tandy showed up with a vice-president from Tandy Company and Jack Shapiro. I laid it right on the line and said somebody had lied to me. They told me how great Giant was doing with financial reports to back their claims, and then the company went belly up.

"Something fraudulent is going on here."

I couldn't back that up, but it couldn't have been anything else. It was like the old Duck Rule. If it looks like a duck, walks like a duck, and quacks like a duck, it's a duck no matter what you call it.

"Just give me back my company."

That was the theme of my presentation as the meeting went on all morning. Tandy was a good listener and when it came time for lunch, Shapiro said, "I know a good place for lunch."

"I don't give a shit where you go, Jack. Charles and I are going to lunch alone," Tandy announced to the stunned and chagrined Shapiro. And we did.

We took a booth in the quiet corner of a little restaurant nearby. Tandy leaned forward to me, and in a conspiratorial tone said, "Charles, I have to tell you something. I like your company."

"So do I. But tell me, why do you like it?"

"Because you use the kiss method!"

He wrote out K I S S on the napkin.

"Never heard of it. What does it mean?"

"K I S S stands for Keep It Simple, Stupid. You may not

know it, Charles, but you are using the Kiss Method. I know you're doing it well and I like it."

He went on to flatter me that I knew how to run a company. He knew that I ran a chain of 37 convenience stores, five ice cream parlours, and a wholesale ice cream business with only 12 people—ONLY 12 people. The problem with Giant was, as I had said all along, too many people doing too little work and getting in each other's way.

Why didn't I see all this coming again? It was the flatter-and-fool approach once more.

"Charles, we're going to straighten Giant out and get them back in business. I know how to do it. I've done it before. You just have a little faith in me. Stay with me on this. When it's all over, I'm going to give you 360,000 shares more than you have now. You deserve it and I'll see that you get it."

Sure, he gave it to me, but it was the shaft and not the shares. I should have known that he was giving me nothing but bullshit. But I couldn't do anything else that day. He wasn't giving me my stores back, and he never did give me 360,000 worthless shares of Giant.

"Well, I still would rather have my company back."

Charles Tandy was in charge of Giant from mid-April to mid-August and just plain liquidated the company. He sold off all the merchandise at 50 cents and then at 40 cents and then 25 cents and then, finally, 10 cents on the dollar and just cashed it out. He got a big fee in the process. I don't think he ever intended rebuilding Giant and getting it back in business. He was a liquidator—not a builder.

After that senseless meeting and lunch, I went to Ford Goldman and we started a legal campaign in bankruptcy court to get my company back. The poor man, I was calling him constantly. Every time we spoke, I bombarded him with questions.

"What's going on? What can I do? What are they telling you?"

I may have made a pest of myself, but I was fighting for my business life. I was fighting to rescue what I had spent 40 years building and was on the edge of oblivion because of thieves, liars, hustlers, and sharks.

It is not my nature to sit idly by. I need to know and I need to do. That's what makes up me: work, action, movement, progress.

When the case finally got to court, the truth came out and it was as I had suspected. Kaufman, Shapiro, Lieberman and Silverstein were crooks. They had doctored the books to change a $2,500,000 loss for 1972 into a $1,300,000 profit. Those doctored books are what the bankers and stockbrokers saw while the four big-shot crooks wheeled and dealed. In truth, at the end of fiscal year, February 1, 1973, Giant Stores had a loss of TEN MILLION plus.

The tricks and gimmicks they used to doctor the books were clever, but deliberately crooked. They would shift inventory of merchandise from store to store just ahead of the visits of outside auditors so the same goods were being counted three, four, and five times. They got suppliers to change the dates on bills so they could be put in different accounting periods.

The list of scams they used was endless. Lieberman was the quarterback of these plays, because he was formerly with the outside accounting firm of Touche Ross and knew what his former colleagues would look for when conducting an audit. The way he could juggle books, he should have been on the Ed Sullivan Show.

I couldn't help but wonder what would have happened if all that energy and talent had been devoted to running the business instead of cheating everyone.

It took until 1976, but the Securities and Exchange Commission [SEC] finally officially disciplined Giant's underwriter for violations in connection with the 1972 Giant stock offering. Later that year, the SEC took legal action against Touche Ross, Giant's former executives and three Giant suppliers involved in the scams.

Touche Ross was subsequently disciplined and paid substantial funds in a class action settlement. The fall guy was Armin J. Frankel, a Touche Ross partner in charge of the Giant audits, who claimed to have been "under stressful conditions" because the Giant executives were threatening to get him fired.

That doesn't explain why the whole Touche Ross firm caved in. I think it was because Benjamin Lieberman knew how to bully the Touche Ross people since he used to work there. He was one of their boys. He knew just exactly how far he could go. He knew exactly what they would do. He knew exactly what they would accept and what they wouldn't.

At the end, the four Giant executives who had lied to me and cheated me were convicted of falsifying financial statements and sent to prison for 4 to 6 months each. I personally was in favor of horsewhipping or perhaps hanging.

None of this made me feel better or made me whole again. These criminals had ruined me. I had sunk everything I had into Dairy Mart except my home. The 43,000 shares of Giant stock they had given me and the 43,000 they were going to give me was worthless.

I had lost a life's work.

In the end, I had nothing.

Actually, that wasn't quite true.

CHAPTER XXVII

Reborn Dairy Mart and Me

AT THE END with Giant, I said I had nothing. Actually, it would be more accurate to say that I had my health, my determination, my wits, and most valuable of all, I had Jan.

Jan has always been there to help, to guide, to steady, and to encourage. If ever a man was blessed with the most wonderful wife in the world, it has been Charlie Nirenberg.

> *I was so sad, not because we lost everything, but because I felt so badly for him. In his lifetime, his dream had come true and he had so many wonderful plans for the future. Then, all of a sudden it all fell apart. If Charlie has control of things and they go wrong, he'll take the blame, but this wasn't his fault.*
>
> —My wife, Jan

Ford Goldman and I tried to get the Giant people to return my stores because we claimed they had stolen them from me by deceit and fraud. They weren't budging. Charles Tandy, my old buddy, couldn't care less. He was hanging on to Dairy Mart if he could because it was one of the few profit-making assets Giant still had.

We brought in a bankruptcy court consultant, George Freedlander, to make our case to the judge. He succeeded in making a deal that would get my company back except for one glitch: it would cost me $200,000. I had been robbed of my company and now I had to pay the thief $200,000!

> *The hardest thing I have ever done was getting his company out of bankruptcy. The great thing in his life was down the drain, and down the drain through no reason of his own.*
>
> *Charlie couldn't do anything about it and he would literally go home, take an ax, and cut down trees and, ultimately, he cleared the property. That was the way he got rid of his frustrations.*
>
> *He would call me at home quite often and vent his frustrations. He would exhaust me. My wife always knew when he called. I said, "Charlie you just have to be patient." Finally, we got his company back.*
>
> *Shortly after Charlie bought his company back my wife and I got a letter from a travel agency saying we were entitled to one week free vacation anywhere in the Caribbean. I immediately declined, but said he could buy us a dinner. The next day he responded saying, "That's wonderful. We'll have dinner at the Plantation Inn in Jamaica," and we spent a week there with Charlie and Jan.*
>
> —My lawyer and long-time friend, Ford Goldman

I had a problem. I didn't have $200,000. So I did what I usually did when I needed money, I went to the bank. I went to the Shawmut First Bank in Springfield, where I had a good reputation, and talked with my friend Frank Barrett.

This was going to be the biggest sales job I had ever undertaken because I would have to prove to Frank that I had something worth $200,000 before he could lend me the money. So I did. I talked, I sold, I proved like I have never done before. I proved it this way and I proved it that way. I proved it up and I proved it down. I proved it left and I proved it right. This was my one chance and I HAD to succeed or I would never get my company back.

Actually, I had a hidden ally in this presentation. It was just like my early days with the 84th Division in World War II where I had to contend with a stupid First Sergeant. Here my secret weapon was the internal auditor who had an I.Q. that compared with Sergeant Kohler's. He couldn't have kept a good set of books for a shoeshine stand.

All during our fight to get Dairy Mart back, this guy kept showing me why Dairy Mart was losing $100,000 a year and was not really worth much. I said nothing at the time, because, as long as they claimed we were losing money, I might get the company back at a lower price. I was right.

When I sat with Frank, I showed him what I thought were realistic figures that had us making money.

"Okay, Charlie, I trust you because we have done business before and you have never lied to me."

He trusted me, but he still double-checked everything I said before agreeing to the loan. Then he went with Ford and me to the bankruptcy court in Boston on December 3, 1973, to close the deal.

Frank sat there holding the bank's check for $200,000 and wouldn't hand it over until the Giant people had signed every document, crossed every "t" and dotted every "i."

Dairy Mart was mine again ten days short of my 50th birthday, and I was determined, on that cold day in December, to look ahead and not backward. I had a future, and the men who cheated me did not. I could not let the people who trusted me down: Frank Barrett at the bank, the loyal people at Dairy Mart, my loving and supportive family.

From April until December, while Ford, George, and I fought to get Dairy Mart back, I endured the most stressful time of my life. I didn't control my stores or my destiny. Each day I waited at the office for a call, but none came. So I would leave at noon and go home to chop trees.

I visualized Ted Kaufman and my ax drove deeply into the log. I saw Shapiro's face in my mind and my ax cut a giant gouge into the wood. Lieberman would appear and a telling whack slashed the timber. Silverstein arose in my head and my ax descended with vicious determination!

Even if I had lost Dairy Mart, I would at least have gained a huge stack of firewood. But I didn't lose Dairy Mart. It was tough, but it was behind me and I didn't seek revenge. I believe in the old country saying that he who seeks revenge should dig two graves, because he will end up destroying his enemy and himself.

I could never have gotten through 1973, tree chopping or not, without Jan. Her strength sustained me. The same faith that she had when we first married and moved to Springfield was there when I needed it. She has been my Rock of Gibraltar, but sometimes even rocks can cry, and one dark, dark day in that awful year, she did.

I took her in my arms and we hugged together while I told her not to worry because everything was going to be all right. I really believed that because I knew from my mother and my own life that determination would win. What my mother had gone through made our crisis pale, but still real to us. I knew I could and would start over and succeed again. Obviously, I got discouraged, too, many times while I was trying to get Dairy Mart back. I HAD to prove that the man they ridiculed could do what they couldn't do.

I might have given up and felt sorry for myself, but that's not an option when you've got three kids, two of whom are in college. It's also not an option when you're me.

A letter from the First National Bank of Boston triggered Jan's tears. It wanted the money we had borrowed against the shares of Giant stock it had lent us.

They had lent money against Giant stock to all the other top Giant executives, too, and now the stock wasn't worth a penny. I had lost over $2 million on the Giant swindle and nobody was going to pay for my loss, but the bank had lost $200,000 on my part of the deal and wanted me to pay for its loss.

As we had done before, Jan and I added up everything we had and it came to $65,000. This wasn't $65,000 we could spare, it was every penny we had. I went into the First National and laid it on the table.

"Fellows, all I have to my name is $65,000. What else can I say or do?"

They took it gladly and wrote off the rest of the note. It's the only time in my life that anyone lost money on me and that's because we were both swindled by the Big Four at Giant. I don't believe any of the other Giant executives made any attempt to settle the notes they owed First National. Did that make me a fool? Maybe and maybe not. It doesn't matter, because it's the way Jan and I are.

Now I had Dairy Mart back, with 37 convenience stores and five ice cream parlours. The past was behind me and the future was ahead. It was actually a great feeling to be my own man again—captain of my ship again.

It was a feeling such as Mark Twain must have had when, hearing his obituary had been mistakenly published, said, "The reports of my death have been greatly exaggerated."

CHAPTER XXVIII

The Dairy with No Milk Cows

IF I HAD been on a football team, I would have been in the locker room pouring champagne over my head. Since I wasn't, I put my head to better use.

It was time for me to undertake two major construction projects for Dairy Mart. One would be to construct a modern headquarters for the future. The other would be to construct a modern headquarters executive staff for the future.

Of course, I didn't have any significant money to do these things, but, what the heck, I did them anyhow.

On the modern headquarters, Ford put me onto the Connecticut Development Authority [CDA] just down Highway 91 from where we were in Springfield, Massachusetts.

We were in Jamaica on one of those little Sunfish boats. We were beyond the reef. They told us not to go beyond the reef, but not Charlie. Charlie saw a better wind out there. He started talking about how he wanted to build his own dairy. Right in the middle of the Caribbean we were talking about industrial bond financing that Connecticut had and Massachusetts didn't. And that's how it started. Our next hurdle was to build this facility.

—Ford Goldman

We found a beautiful, pastoral industrial park in Enfield right by Highway 91 that was an ideal location. Both Enfield and Connecticut were anxious to have us come across the border and settle with them. The CDA had available some new industrial bonds Ford told me about, which would make financing the construction possible at a very low interest rate.

All I had to do was come up with $600,000 to buy the land and the down payment and it would be possible. Of course, I didn't have $600,000. I didn't have $60,000, but I had an idea about how to get it through creative financing.

My British friend, David Harper, had run my five Princess Ice Cream Parlours into the ground in the year and a half he was managing them. He used the cheapest products he could find. I had been running a top quality restaurant serving top quality food because I was looking for repeat business. So I immediately set about reviving them when I got them back.

Having done that, I was now ready to franchise the five Princess Ice Cream Parlours in order to raise the necessary downpayment of $600,000 for my dairy plant.

The reasons I wanted to build this dairy plant were several fold. First, the plant would buy milk from farmers and process it into fresh farm milk for our Dairy Mart stores. Having my own plant would give me better quality control. Secondly, I needed a new and impressive corporate headquarters building.

Also, I learned way back in the days I was selling eggs in front of the family farm in Millis that I made more profit selling eggs from my own chickens than selling eggs I had bought from other chicken farmers. So, I could make more profit making my own bottled milk and dairy products than by buying them from someone else.

Finally, I think it was psychological—both private and public. I had just recovered from an extremely long fight in which some people thought Dairy Mart had gone bankrupt—it hadn't —and both my private spirit and my public image were battered and bruised. Making a giant step—no, I don't mean that; the last Giant step had almost destroyed me—making a big step forward would restore my private confidence and would enhance Dairy Mart's public image.

So naturally I went to see my friendly banker, Frank Barrett, to run my plan by him. I told him I wanted a combination office building and milk processing plant and how low cost development money was available from the CDA. It was going to be a $2.5 million project and I needed $600,000 downpayment to get the rest of the money from CDA. Frank's coy question, as if he didn't already know why I was there to see him, was, "How are you going to get the money for the downpayment on the $2.5 million project?"

"The Princess Parlours. I own them outright, and I'm going to franchise the five of them for $600,000."

"How is that going to work?"

"I'll sell each franchise to a good manager whom I have trained and will stand behind. He will come to you and borrow the franchise price to be paid off over several years."

"Except that those are not the kind of notes we want to have, Charlie. If one of them defaults, the bank is in the ice cream parlour business and we don't want that."

"That's why I will cosign their notes to you. If they default, I'll step in and take back the ice cream parlour, and you know I know how to run one."

"But, Charlie, you're borrowing the downpayment."

"Not really, because I am putting up the equity in the five Snow White Princess Parlours."

"But you're not putting up any of your own money for the downpayment."

"Actually, Frank, I am putting up something of value—my equity in the five Snow White Princess Parlours. You're converting it into cash for the downpayment."

I finally made my point and Frank went along with the plan. This is what's called creative financing, and if you think about it, it's very creative. In essence I was guaranteeing the notes for money that was being paid to me. Little matter, Frank went for it. I soon had my $600,000 and the project was under way.

When we came into the Enfield Industrial Park, it was just farm land, which fit perfectly with my concept. The building was an office with a barnlike look, complete with a silo. I wanted a farm setting because I was building a milk farm and not a milk factory. In those early days, there were cattle grazing in nearby fields, which added to the charm. People would say, "Isn't it wonderful? You have your own cows across the street and you process their milk over here."

I just smiled and never explained the difference between beef steers and milk cows. It didn't matter because, anyway, I loved coming to work in that peaceful setting. It was quite a change from what life had been like the year before.

When I built the Enfield plant, I only had 40 stores. Nobody in his right mind would build a plant for just 40 stores, but nobody ever said I was in my right mind. I had a vision. I knew there would be more Dairy Mart stores, but I didn't talk about it much except to Jan. My vision was for 1,000 Dairy Mart stores.

The success of the dairy plant, which became profitable within six months, reaffirmed that I knew what I was doing, and I pushed ahead opening stores as fast as I could.

With the new plant finished and in operation, it was time for me to turn to my next major construction job. It was time for me to construct an executive staff for the future.

CHAPTER XXIX

Putting Together a Winning Team

I HAD A little time on my hands while the new plant was still under construction, and as I made plans for acquiring more stores, I realized I could not do it alone anymore. Although I had lost a couple of million dollars in the Giant Store fiasco, I had gained something, too. With every failure, every loss, there is always something you gain, something you learn. What I had learned from Giant was an understanding of organizational necessity. Their organization was, in my mind, much too deep. Too many chiefs for the number of Indians. But I did recognize the need for some really key people to surround the chief executive. And I decided that the number one person on the list of key people for Dairy Mart at that point and time was someone to keep the numbers straight. We needed a chief financial officer.

Since Larry Handler, of Arthur Andersen & Co., was the one who had first taken all the bits and pieces of paper and turned them into a financial statement for me, he was the first one to come to mind. He had continued on as manager of the Dairy Mart account and knew the figures like no one I could think of. I had learned to trust and depend upon him even though he was not an employee. Still, he had been the one I had turned to for financial advice for more than four years.

So I approached him about joining me for lunch in the winter of 1974. Larry, being the ethical gentleman that he is, said, "Charlie, if you're thinking about asking me to join your company, it would be a conflict of interest for me to discuss it with you. But I am giving serious consideration to going into industry, and if I decide to do that, I will be in touch with you. I expect to make that decision on April 1 of this year." He was also methodical.

With Larry Handler, that meant April 1. Not April 2. Not March 31. You could bet money on it. And sure enough, on April 1, I got a call from Larry and he said, "I am ready to have lunch with you."

As a result, he joined Dairy Mart at a salary not too much higher than Arthur Andersen had been paying him. I believe the figure was $25,000 a year. However, before he left Dairy Mart, he was well into a six-figure salary and had handsome stock options. But I was offering him both a challenge and an opportunity he didn't have, and this can be important to a young man who wants to get ahead in the business world.

Perhaps even more important, the day we had lunch I proceeded to outline my vision of what I wanted to do with the company and show him what I had in mind for the future. He liked what he heard. He liked what he saw. He liked the challenge. He liked the thought of being the number two man in the company. Still, he said, "I am not going to accept your offer today, but I expect to make a decision on this by July 1."

All of these things are very important to the character of Larry Handler. He is a very precise and exacting individual. But as precise and exacting as he is, he called me on June 27. This indicated to me that he really wanted to go to work for Dairy Mart. And this also indicated to me that he was the type of key player I wanted on my team.

He gave Arthur Andersen 30 days notice and joined my company on August 1, 1974; so I had the first member of the key team I was going to put together. He wasn't someone I had hired from putting an ad in the paper and interviewing. I knew what he could do, because he had been working for me for over four years. I knew exactly what I was getting.

In Larry's case, he had already proven himself on numerous occasions. He started as Assistant Treasurer [my wife was

Treasurer] and he was from day one an asset to Dairy Mart. He would go on to become a truly great chief financial officer.

With my financial house in order, I needed money for growth. I turned my attention to finding the key someone who could head up operations. After your financial man gets the money and the growth occurs, you need someone to run the stores.

As even today, I preferred to promote from within; so I started looking around for the right person to relieve me of the day-to-day job of operations. After considering several people, a young man by the name of Steve Montgomery stood out. He was an aggressive manager who had started out with one Dairy Mart store but now had two stores. He had graduated from college with a degree in marketing and was a very impressive conversationalist. So I brought him in for a talk.

After mostly listening to him, I thought to myself: this guy has the innate talent it is going to take for the man who takes over operations. So I said to him, "Steve, how would you like to go to work for Dairy Mart here in the home office and give your two stores back?"

I went on to explain that I could not offer him a great deal of money at the time—it was only $12,000 a year. However, like Larry, he was well into a six-figure salary, plus stock options, when he left. But yet again like Larry, I could offer Steve a great future. So he accepted my offer with enthusiasm.

Steve started with the title of Director of Operations, and at that point I had two top men on my key team.

With Steve, the talent was there, but it was still hidden, so I had to start molding him and coaching him and guiding him. I had to channel his talent and his energy. This, of course, is one of the roles of a chief executive officer.

For example, Steve could, and sometimes would, talk without stopping or interruption for as long as two or three hours. This can be both an asset and a liability, so I had to talk to him about this. Coach him a bit. I had him come to my office and I told him that I had noticed he was sometimes on the telephone talking to a store manager for as long as an hour. I wasn't so much worried about running up the telephone bill as I was about his wasting his time and the time of the manager. It also meant he could not talk to as many managers at the end of the day. After explaining this, I gave him a three-minute hour glass egg timer, told him to put it on his desk beside his telephone, and suggested he use it every time he made or received a call. When the three minutes was up, he should figure out a way to close the conversation.

He was a little upset with me for doing this, but it was probably one of the best lessons Steve ever learned. It was the main reason he eventually became an excellent operations manager.

Then in June of 1976, just as we were about to move into our new $2.6 million plant and home office, I got a call from another young man I had been dealing with for some three or four years, and it started me to thinking.

The young man's name was Frank Colaccino. Up until that time, he used to come in to try and sell me real estate, and I was impressed with him. He was only about 21 years old and was working for White Realty at the time.

Here I was when he first started coming in, just trying to recover from my days with Giant Stores and not having any money to work with, but Frank was persistent and he was such a pleasant guy that I took time to listen to him. It was my fault he kept coming in, because I never told him I didn't have any money to buy real estate. Instead, I would listen and then tell him the price was too high.

If he would tell me about a piece of land or property that was listed at $60,000, I would tell him, "Frank, if you can get it for me for $30,000, I just might take it." He sometimes had a deal at a really great location, so great I felt I could not pass it up, and at a price I felt I had to take to the bank. They, too, would often agree that it was a great buy. So I had bought some real estate that way. I didn't have any money to buy it any other way. But I never let Frank know this. I always put up a good front. Always a positive front, I never acted like I couldn't do it.

Frank always came in with a beautiful smile on his face, and I was impressed with his persistence. He never gave up. And every now and then, we would do some business.

As I got to know him better as time went by, I found that Frank had accomplished things by his early twenties that people in their early eighties had never accomplished.

So one day when he came in to try and sell me some more

real estate, I said to him, "Frank, you know, someday you are going to come to work for me." He just smiled that big smile of his, but didn't say a word.

In June of 1976, Frank called me up one day and made an appointment to see me, just as he had done so many times in the past. When I got home that night, I told Jan that Frank had called me but I had a hunch he wasn't coming by to sell real estate this time. I told her, "He is ready to go to work for us. I just feel it."

Sure enough, the day he came in, he started with, "You know, Charlie, you told me that I was going to go to work for you someday, and I am ready if you are." It was no surprise, but I had a problem and had to say to him, "Frank, we just put every nickel we have into this plant and office building. You couldn't have come along at a worse time. But Frank, I told you that you could come to work for me and I will keep my word. The only problem I have right now is that I don't know how I am going to pay you. But tell me, how much money did you make with White Realty last year?"

He said, "With all my commissions, I made about $12,000." I said, "If you feel you can start with me for $12,000, we have a deal. And let me tell you something, Frank, you are going to go a long way with this company."

Today, Frank is President and Chief Executive Officer and is running the company. And he did it in 16 years.

When he started to work for Dairy Mart, I really didn't know what to do with him. I just knew he was the kind of dynamic person the company needed.

Of course, he knew real estate, how to sell it and the value of it, so I decided to give him a good challenge right off the bat. I said, "Frank, we are growing as fast as we can, but money is tight. When we build a new store for $250,000, do you think you could go out and sell someone on a lease-back deal at $250,000 for the store, with a clause that would allow us to buy it back at the end of ten years? We will sign a lease for ten years, so they will make money off of us and then get all of their money back when the lease is up."

"Sure, I can do that, Charlie," was his answer. And he went out and did it. He discovered that there were a lot of doctors and other professional people looking for a tax shelter of this type. It paid them more money than any bank interest, and they could amortize the $250,000 and write it off on their income tax returns.

He started out in charge of real estate and new construction, and as time went by, I gave him the title Director of Corporate Development. Now my team of key people had grown to three.

That was in 1976. In seven years I would add one more key man to my executive team, but it is more appropriate for me to tell that story in a chapter coming up soon.

The family in 1960.

With Yitzhak Rabin, the Prime Minister of Israel.

Me in the milk plant as shown in Barron's Weekly (1984).

Talking to potential investors in Dairy Mart stock, (1983).

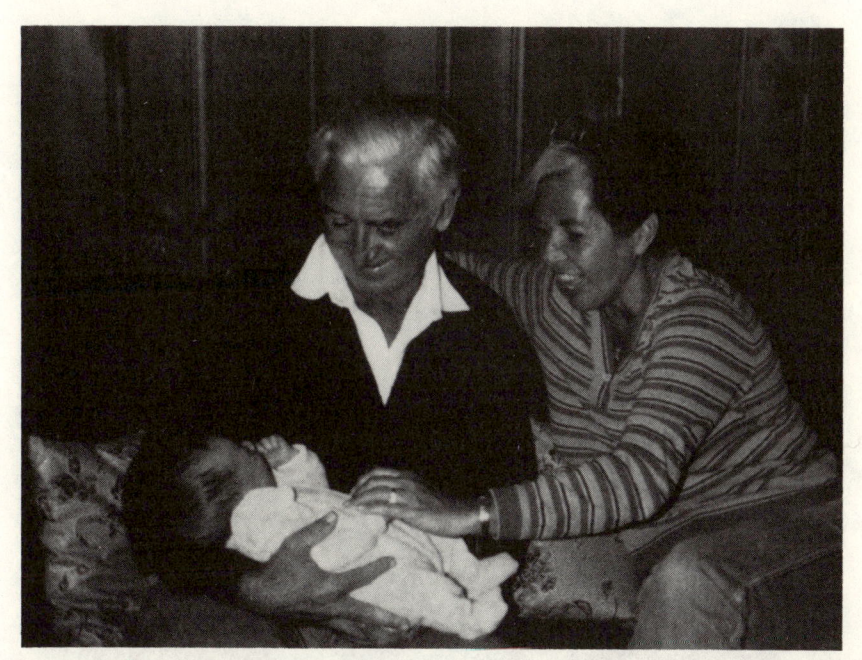

Jan and I admiring our week-old first grandchild, Joshua (1984).

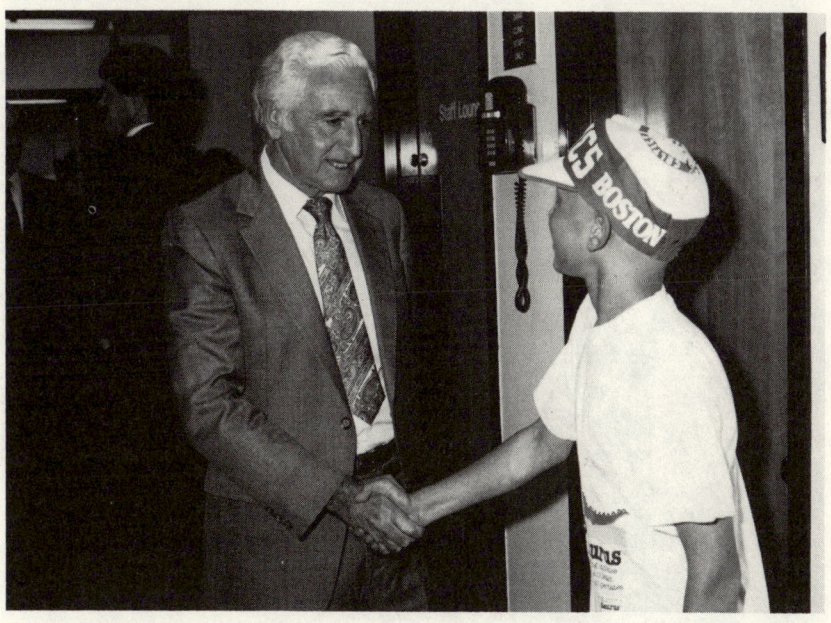

Helping hand to one of the young people helped by the Jimmy Fund.

Frank Colaccino
President and Chief Executive Officer

Mitchell J. Kupperman
Executive Vice President
Human Resources

Gregory G Landry
Executive Vice President
Chief Financial Officer

Robert B. Stein, Jr.
Executive Vice President
Store Operations
and General Manager

The new Dairy Mart management team.

(Left to right) Larry Handler, Frank Alger and me.

Steve Montgomery in January, 1985.

Me and Carl Yastrzemski doing a Jimmy Fund TV spot.

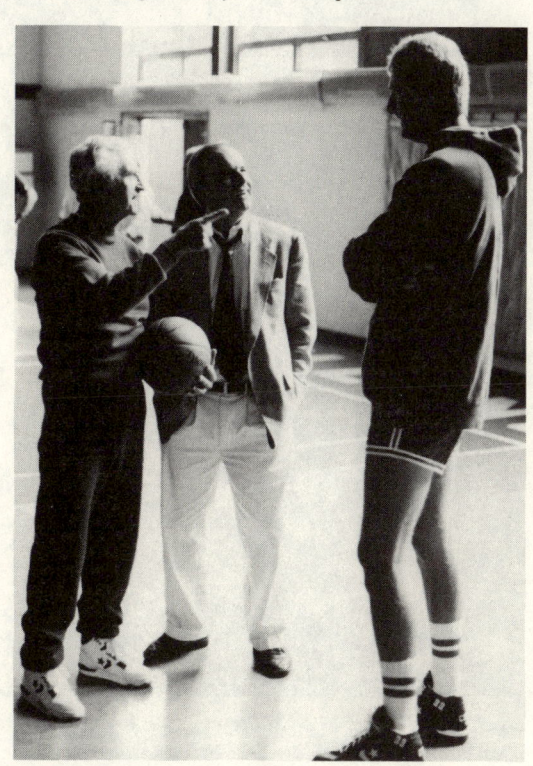

(Left to right) Me, advertising man Rob LaChance, and basketball star, Larry Bird.

Me as the quarter catchers for the Jimmy Fund.

(Left to right) Me; Mike Andrews of the Jimmy Fund; announcer, Ken Coleman; Red Sox Pitcher, Bob Stanley; and, Frank Colaccino helping out the Jimmy Fund.

Jan, me and President Jerry Ford.

President Reagan and me.

Ground-breaking of Dairy Mart farm facility with city officials and Connecticut Development Authority officials.

A snowy day at our new Enfield offices and plant.

CHAPTER XXX

Building by Buying

We finished the Enfield office and plant in 1976 when we had 40 stores, and, with my new management team in operation four years later, we were close to the 100 mark.

Every thing was growing nicely. By 1980 we were approaching the 100 mark. I had every reason to be content and happy, but I got to thinking. I had been in the convenience store business since 1962—some 18 years. This meant I was only averaging around five and a half stores a year.

I was 56 years old in 1980, so that meant I would be around 75 years old before I reached the next plateau of having 200 stores. Since I still harbored the goal of eventually having 1,000 stores, I was going to be older than Methuselah before I reached that goal.

The realization that building five and a half new stores a year wasn't the formula for reaching 1,000 in my lifetime happened about the time Leon Cornell dropped by to see me.

I had missed buying the 66 Sunnybrook stores in Rhode Island because Giant Stores didn't act on my recommendation, and Leon got them instead.

"You know, Charlie, I would like to buy your company."

"Well, Leon, everything is for sale at Dairy Mart, but you may find the price a bit steep."

"How so?"

"I have just completed a new milk plant and am about to reach 100 stores. I'm in a growth mood, not a selling mood..."

"I see, well..."

"But I am always willing to talk. I'm a businessman and, who knows, if you can't buy me, maybe I can buy you."

That's exactly what this interesting and colorful Leon Cornell wanted to hear. He wanted to sell, but didn't dare admit it openly because it would weaken his bargaining position.

He was a golf nut who always had his clubs and shoes in the trunk of his Ferrari ready to play. His businessman father had left him a good dairy business. Leon was smart enough to see Sunnybrook Farms as a good investment, but didn't have the discipline to run it.

We got around to negotiating and it came down to this: after checking all 66 stores and going over the books, 40 of the stores were okay but needed to be upgraded, and the other 26 were bad. The deal was a little sweeter because Leon owned 12 of the locations outright. Larry and I figured it still came down to $1.5 million as an opening bid. Leon countered with $1.6 and then, before we could answer, raised it to $1.7.

Larry was opposed, but my gut feeling was that, even if we overpaid then, the 12 owned parcels would correct our mistake in time. We made the deal and ten years later, the 12 parcels alone were worth $1.7 million.

We took over the chain in November of 1980 and ended up with the two managers Leon had running the stores on our payroll. Our people looked at the way they were operating Sunnybrook's stores and quickly realized why they were not doing very well. While Leon Cornell was busy playing golf, his two Sunnybrook managers were busy wheeling and dealing with the suppliers, and they were wheeling and dealing in a way that we do not tolerate at Dairy Mart. I knew they had to go and soon found the way.

About a month after we took over, it was Christmas bonus time, but there were no bonus checks for the two Sunnybrook managers. They had been with us roughly 30 days, so I took the stand that any bonus should come from Leon for whom they had been working a long time. And Leon could not think of any good reason why he should give them a bonus for the poor job they had done for him.

Then on New Year's Eve, I had a call from the two and their message was brief and terse: "Come pick up the keys. We are leaving." That was fine with me, although it was a bit difficult to take over from them on New Year's Day. But I had some of our people run over to Rhode Island and they were gone. They had saved me doing what I was going to have to do the first of the year anyway.

The 40 good stores continued operating all right, so I went to work on what to do with the 26 that were losing money. Six were so bad, we just closed them.

As for the remaining 20, experience solved the problem for me. I had learned one of the most critical business lessons years ago back on the Millis farm. When I was selling chickens to the butcher, I could get more money for them if I kept them a month longer. However, at 12, I figured out that the cost of another month's feed was more than the extra money I earned. So I sold them earlier.

I learned it was better to put money where it pays the best return. It is wiser to spend time and money on a good store and make it a better store than to spend time and money on trying to salvage a loser.

The owner of the East Greenwich Dairy who had been selling bottled milk to Sunnybrook called me about continuing to supply those stores. It was a golden opportunity. I couldn't do the business with him that he wanted, but maybe I could the business with him that I wanted.

I explained we had 20 marginal stores he could probably turn into good producers because he could devote more time to developing them that I could. I didn't mislead him, but the thought of having 20 stores of his own was appealing, even if he couldn't supply my remaining stores with milk since we had our own plant. He bought the 20 stores from me and, for some reason of his own, hired those same two Sunnybrook managers to run them.

So, we were on our way buying up stores. By the end of 1981

we had 148; we made another small acquisition in 1982; and, in 1983 we were preparing to take over the Dutchland Farms chain of 34 stores.

We were moving, and it was exciting.

CHAPTER XXXI

Two Conversations

In 1983, I had two important conversations that affected the direction of the company and my life.

One decision involved a sensitive area for me, my family. My attitude was that, if any member of my family wanted a job, it was here for them, but it came with no guarantees. Your family connection could get you in the door, but your family connection wouldn't keep you there if you didn't do the job.

My son, Larry, followed the course his older sister had and went off to college and to play around before he settled down to something serious. That is probably the American way for the second generation, but it was certainly not a luxury I ever had and maybe that gave me a less than charitable view of it.

Afterward, Larry decided he loved skiing and took to hanging around New England ski resorts having a good time and occasionally picking up a little work here or there.

Ultimately, he wearied of that and returned to Springfield and went to work for Dairy Mart. It made us both a little nervous, because everybody knew what the relationship was and everybody was watching to see if the kid would screw up or if Dad would make it too easy or if this or if that. And we were both very conscious of the other one in our own private way.

Larry started in the blow-mold room of the plant. One of the things we do in the plant is to take milk or juices or other drinks in bulk and bottle them into quart, half-gallon, and gallon plastic containers.

As part of the process, we shape or mold raw plastic into plastic bottles on an enormously fast assembly line. The place where we do that is, cleverly, called "the blow-mold room." That's where Larry worked for a couple of years.

After a while, I thought it might be time for Larry to get some retail experience. I don't know if I was thinking about his learning the business with an idea of someday moving into management or not, but you could never tell. So when the manager's slot opened up at The Dairy Mart Farm store, I offered it to Larry and he took it.

I'm not sure why Larry took it and he probably isn't sure either. The motives and meanings between us are complicated, as they are with most parents and children. The thing that troubled me deep down in my private father's heart was that I was proud of my son and I wanted to reach out to him, but it seemed so hard sometimes. It seemed as if he didn't want me to know him and yet, that he yearned for us to be closer.

The specter that haunted me in this relationship was that same one that must have haunted my own father, with a twist. My father was never able to embrace his dreams of success and was overshadowed in some ways by his own son. In the instance of Larry and me, it was the reverse. And, like my daughters who were leery of being the cookie cutter children of a prominent, successful businessman, Larry was fearful of being compared with me and concerned he wouldn't attain what I had. He didn't want to be Mr. Dairy Mart, Junior. He wanted to be his own man.

Whatever the feelings and reasoning, Larry didn't like being a Dairy Mart manager and, when there was another opening in the blow-mold room, asked to go back there. He did that, but in time left Dairy Mart to strike out on his own. That turned out to be a good move, because he has become a very successful real estate man.

In retrospect, I think we were both the better for Larry's striking out on his own. We do better as father and son than we do as work colleagues.

Given all that, I wasn't prepared for the conversation I had with Mitch Kupperman, my daughter Sandi's husband, on the road to Cape Cod one afternoon in 1983.

"You know, I'm about to get my Ph.D. and I would like to come to work for your company."

"Is that really necessary, Mitch?"

He didn't say anything, so I continued.

"I'm going to level with you. I didn't spend a lifetime building a company so that my kids couldn't get a job. You can have a job anytime you want one, but I must tell you that you are not starting with a big salary and you'll have an uphill battle with some of the people in the company."

"I know that, but I look at it as a great opportunity. I don't expect or want special treatment. Just give me a chance and I'll prove my worth and earn my pay. There are other places I could go, but you have a company that can use what I have to offer and I am enthusiastic about helping Dairy Mart grow."

So, in late 1983 Mitch joined the company as an executive without title and very quickly was given the shunning treatment by the other executives. To his credit, he didn't fight back or quit. Instead, he got me to let him try straightening out problems we were having with our Rhode Island stores.

He went there and created a human resources operation he called a People Bank that made it possible to re-staff our stores with effective and happy employees. The result was that the stores' service improved and so did the bottom line. That's when Mitch got the call from Steve Montgomery. "I don't know what you're doing out there, but it seems to be working. How about doing it back here?"

Suddenly, Mitch wasn't my son-in-law to Steve any more. He was a productive member of the management team. That's how he became the fourth member of my management team, as Director of Human Resources.

The other conversation I had in 1983 that affected me and the company was with Bill Robbins of an old-line, regional investment banking firm, Advest, headquartered in Hartford.

Bill and I had talked over the years about a public stock offering, but never connected until after I had made the Sunnybrook acquisition and was getting ready to purchase Dutchland.

"Maybe now is the time to go public, Charlie. Let's put something together and take a look at it."

We were growing and looking good, with a $400,000 net for 1982, and those are the two things that get investment bankers' noses twitching.

Things were going well, and I was getting financing from Fleet Bank for these new acquisitions, but there is a Chain Belt of Opportunity that I didn't want to miss. In business, opportunities keep coming along just like they're on a chain belt. When they're in front of you, you either take them off or you lose them. I had seen too many opportunities go by and I decided not to let it happen again. We went for a public offering.

The deal was that we would offer 360,000 shares at somewhere between $7.00 and $9.00. I figured $8.00 would be the minimum. The Company would sell 300,000, and I would sell 60,000 personally. Naturally, the underwriting broker wanted the lowest price possible, because it's easier to sell and makes his floor guarantee easier.

The attorneys were busy preparing the prospectus and the accountants were finalizing the financial statements. Both fields pay very good money, and we soon had around $300,000 in attorney and accountant fees.

The package they prepared then went to the Securities and Exchange Commission [SEC]. The people there examined it carefully for about four weeks before they came back with their comments. As always, the SEC wanted a change here and a change there, which led to discussions between the SEC and our attorneys and accountants. So it was at least six weeks before the SEC was satisfied and everyone of us involved breathed a sigh of relief. All this is standard procedure for the government. It takes its time, as it should.

Now, the investment banking house was asked to say something like, "Let's see. We will be ready on Monday, but maybe Monday is not the best day. Let's try it Wednesday. And then, someone else will say that Tuesday is the best morning to come out with an offering." So it is changed again. At least that's the way it went for Dairy Mart.

On Monday morning we had one more meeting of the principals who had been involved, to negotiate the price of the stock that was to be issued the following morning.

John Everetts and Bill Robbins represented Advest and Larry Handler and I represented Dairy Mart. Everetts began, "Well, Charlie, what do you think it should be?"

"It should be nine dollars."

"Wow! I'm here to tell you there's no way you're going to get nine, Charlie. I don't mean to insult you, but let's get real. The best I can see is around seven."

"John, you asked me and I told you. We should get at least nine dollars."

"How do you figure?"

"This Dutchland deal is going to have the stock past nine in a hurry. Come on, John, you and I both know it's worth more than seven."

There followed a lot of general discussion—mostly baloney—while each side tried to wear down the other. Finally, John, as a good salesman, tried to close the deal.

"I'll tell you what I'm going to do, Charlie, I'm going to give you eight dollars and that's it."

He didn't smile when he said it and I didn't smile when I answered. It was high noon and we were facing off.

"I'm going to tell you something and I want you to get it straight. I am not going to fool with you any longer. Eight-fifty is the price. That's what I really wanted all along and that's what I intend to get."

"Eight dollars is it."

"You're wasting my time."

I picked up my papers and walked out of the room, while Larry was turning blue because we had $300,000 invested in the public offering.

Everetts and Robbins walked on each side of me as I went down the hall to the elevator jabbering away like couple of magpies, so I figured the deal wasn't lost. But at this point I knew I could get more and that's the important secret of bargaining.

I've known Charlie most of his adult life and it's been interesting how he's changed over the years. He has matured and changed dramatically during that time. At first, he was the typical demanding and tough entrepreneur, but with time he has mellowed and become easier to work with.

Charlie's greatest strength is knowing how to deal with people and motivate them. He is a delight to work with, most generous, but always drives a hard bargain.
—Jerry Hassett, Charlie's Tax Accountant

I walked out of their building and across the street to my attorney's office.

"Ford, John Everetts wants to give me eight dollars a share and I just walked out on him. I want eight-fifty. He won't budge and neither will I."

The phone rang on Ford's desk.

"I don't know who in the hell your client thinks he is, but he's crazy! We're ready to take him public tomorrow morning and he walked out on us."

"I've been Charlie Nirenberg's legal advisor for a long, long time, but I don't give him business advice."

Tuesday morning came and people were calling asking when we were coming out with the stock. I told them to hang around. At ten o'clock John Everetts was on the phone.

"Can I come up to Enfield and take you to lunch?"

"Sure, John, I'd like to have lunch with you."

He picked me up in his little sports car and we started out the Dairy Mart driveway.

"Which way do we go, right or left?"

"Do you want a slow lunch or a fast lunch?"

"Slow lunch."

"Turn right."

Now I knew we were about to make a deal.

Predictably, the first hour of lunch was devoted to telling me that I was crazy. I agreed, saying the stock was actually worth ten or eleven dollars. The next hour was devoted to telling me how wonderful I was, how wonderful Dairy Mart was, and how wonderful Advest was. Finally, after two hours of bull, we agreed on $8.25 a share. That added up to an additional $90,000.

So I spent a couple of hours, got a free lunch and $90,000. It pays to be persistent.

The stock opened at $8.25. An hour later it was at $9.00. Two hours later, $10.00. It closed at $11.00. For the next three months, it was never under $10.00.

He took to being a public company like a fish to water. He appreciated what was necessary—his responsibility to the stockholders. He realized that they needed value and they weren't going to be happy unless the stock moved up. Unlike many executives today, the Board had to implore him to get his salary up. He felt everybody would do better the more profit there was for the stockholders.

—Ford Goldman

Dairy Mart got $2,475,000 for growth and I got $495,000 for the shares I sold, which was the first time I made any real, hard touch-and-taste money from Dairy Mart.

Now that we were a public company, we needed to think more seriously about our public image, and that meant television.

CHAPTER XXXII

Doing the Television Commercials

WE DID A television commercial with Larry Bird last year that was a real hit. I did two 30-second commercials: In one, I was playing basketball and really getting it through the hoop just like Larry does. Of course, people still think I had a double but I'm not going to tell anybody. You'll have to guess what that really was.

The second one, and that was the real fun ad, was one where I challenged Larry for some one-on-one and he's out there on the basketball court and I come out in my tennis outfit and a tennis racket. Here he is on the basketball court twirling that big basketball with one finger and I look at Larry and say,

"Well, you ready, Larry?"

And, he looks at me and, I'm telling you, his eyes tell a story. Then I look at the basketball and say, "Hey, that's a pretty big ball there, Larry."

And, I've got to tell you that commercial has made a hit all over the place. Coming out in a tennis outfit on a basketball court really did it.

Then, I did a nice commercial with Carl Yastrzemski and I'm pretty proud of it because it was for the Jimmy Fund, one of my main charities, it was for fund raising and that's my pride and joy.

Carl Yastrzemski is up at bat and he's hitting quarters to the outfield and I gotta tell you this guy is so strong, he's actually hitting the quarters right over the fence—the center field wall. And, I'm out there in the outfield with a Jimmy Fund canister trying to catch these quarters.

Well, you can just imagine somebody trying to catch a quarter way out in the outfield, but, again, the quarter clangs into my Jimmy Fund canister. Carl keeps hitting and he asks me, "How am I doing, Charlie?"

"A little more to the left, Carl, a little more to the left."

And, he finally says, "There's gotta be a better way to do this."

And, I say, "Ye, there is." And, I drop a quarter into the Jimmy Fund cannister. "The easy way."

So, these are the kind of ads that I have done. They're all rather humorous. Talking about being humorous, I guess the humorous fellow that I did the ad with is Norm Crosby. Norm came out to do an ad with me for both the Jimmy Fund and the Dairy Mart.

Let me sort of give you the one he did for the Jimmy Fund. He's up there at the counter with a dozen empty drinks there and I said, "Norm, a little thirsty today?"

And, he looked at me and says, "You know, I heard that you give a donation to the Jimmy Fund for every drink that we buy. So, I'm trying to make a donation."

"Yeah, but if you're not so thirsty, Norm, you could have put a quarter in this canister instead."

He says, "Now, you tell me."

And he asks me quietly, as he whispers in my ear and people already know what that whisper is—"Where's the men's room?" And, I tell him, "In the back, Norm, in the back."

And, by the way, he didn't "consume the drinks." He said he "consummated" the drinks.

They're fun ads and I think I enjoyed doing them as much as they did. And, of course, all this started back in 1984, after we'd gone public and we began to realize that we needed more professionalism in our television advertising.

We called in about a dozen different agencies and interviewed them all with our executive team. There was one that seemed to stand out head and shoulders above the others. The ads that this group presented just grabbed you more! They were funny. They were humorous. They had a lot of oomph! They weren't just plain ads that told about a product. People don't always listen to that. They were real exciting ads.

So, after interviewing the dozen agencies, we called this one back. At that time, it was called the La Chance Agency. Today it's Tin Can Alley. A young man by the name of Rob La Chance came with his father, Bob La Chance.

Rob just kept talking, and what I didn't realize was that Rob WAS the real executive there. His father only accompanied him because he was really starting new and he wanted to look like a bigger agency than he was.

After hearing young Rob talk so much, I said to him, "Why don't you keep quiet and let your dad talk for a while?" So his dad started talking, but the poor guy really didn't know that much. Young Rob had to go back in and tell the story again. I've never forgotten it, and Rob has never forgotten it, and Rob's father whom I have seen just recently, still hasn't forgotten it.

After we gave him the bid and said, "Okay, you're going to be our agency. When can you come in with some new television advertising? How long do you need?" He said, "Can you give me a couple of weeks?" I said, "That's fair."

Two weeks later he came back with some story boards—three or four of them. In each of them, there's this gray-haired dude who seems to be prominent among the pictures. I finally looked at him and said, "Tell me, Rob, who's this guy here . . . who's this gray-haired dude?" He says, "That's YOU!" I said, "ME?" I said, "I never did any television advertising. I wasn't even a good dramatist in a high school drama play or anything like that. It's just not me. I don't think I can do it." He says, "I think you can. I think that's the best way for you to advertise."

I said, "Well, let's bring in the executive team and see what they think. They all came in, and looked at the story boards. They said, "We like it. We think you can do it."

"Well, I am afraid that I may not do a good job and disappoint you guys, but if you think I can do it, I'll take a try at it."

That was back in 1984, and I can tell you that, since that time, I think I have done a minimum of thirty different commercials that have played in eleven states from as far north as Massachusetts and as far south as Kentucky.

The latest commercial I did was the airplane commercial with me in a World War I biplane with the old-time helmet and goggles on.

There are people out there having a cook-out and they have their hamburgers and their hot dogs and the kid says to his dad, "Hey, dad, we forgot the Coke®." And, all of a sudden they look up and a whole half-gallon of Coke® just drops down in front of them. They can't figure out where it's from and they look up and there's Charlie Nirenberg up in an airplane delivering Coke®. He drops down a Coke® to this family that needed Coke®.

The kid looks up and points to me in the plane and asks, "Hey, dad, what's that?"

That's me up there delivering the Coke® or ice cream or potato chips or anything that people may need. This is how that ad runs and, when they look up at me, my line is, "They don't call me The Convenience Store Baron for nothing."

That's that same picture you see on the cover of this book. People continue to ask me, "Were you really up there flying that plane?" And, I respond, "What do you think?"

Today, when I travel to Cleveland, Ohio; Louisville, Kentucky; and places that I was never known before, people look at me and say, "You're that guy from Dairy Mart." And I say, "Aw, come on now."

I can't forget that in Cleveland, I always go to the National Car Rental Agency to get a car. I hand them my card and don't tell them who I am. I just say, "I need a car." Before I mention my name, they look at me and say, "You're that guy from Dairy Mart." I say, "Just fill out the card, please don't kid with me." "No, no, no. I'm really not kidding."

"Well, if you're really not kidding, tell me an ad that I'm in." They can rattle it off verbatim. I can't believe it, but that's how effective those ads were. They rattle it off verbatim.

When they finally get my car, I go outside to get into the bus and the bus driver says, "You're that guy from Dairy Mart!" So I've got to tell you that it's not just in Enfield, Connecticut, that I'm known. People in the greater part of 11 states know Charlie Nirenberg as the guy they see on TV—the guy that's the image of Dairy Mart. The Colonel Sanders of Dairy Mart, if you will.

So I was about to hit 60 and was in a nice liquid cash position. Damn! I gotta tell you, after all I had been through, that felt good!

CHAPTER XXXIII

The Tale of the Whale

THE BIGGEST DEAL of my life came along when I was 62, and the worst thing about it was people calling me "Guppy."

This was a time when the experiences, mistakes, lessons, and perceptions of a lifetime came into focus on the deal everyone thought impossible. It began with a routine conversation between Frank Colaccino and Bucky Brown as Frank was tracking down White Hen Pantries in 1984.

American Stores of Salt Lake City purchased Jewel Tea Company, a supermarket chain out of Chicago, that also owned a chain of convenience stores, White Hen Pantries. There are about 300 of them, primarily located in the Midwest, with about 50 in New England.

Frank was tracking down the information on the White Hen Pantries and contacted the investment bankers for American Stores, Shearson Lehman. He ended up talking with Bucky Brown.

Frank told Bucky who he was and about his role in making the company grow. He told Bucky he knew about American Stores buying Jewel Tea and had heard they were now trying to spin off White Hen Pantries. He said we would be interested in the White Hen Pantries located in New England.

As it turned out, American Stores sold White Hen Pantries to its own management as part of a leveraged buy-out. However, Frank and Bucky developed a very good relationship and would talk two or three times a week on the phone during the several months they were trying to make something out of the White Hen deal.

Finally, they were on the phone one day and Bucky said, "Listen, we're not going to make it. White Hen Pantries, we're not going to do it."

He explained why.

"But we have a property that might be available, because we're also the investment bankers for Sara Lee. We have a convenience store chain that they've decided to sell."

"Yeah, tell me about it."

"It's probably too big for you, but it's a 700-store chain in the Midwest."

"Where?"

"Well, I can't tell you."

"Well, okay, but whereabouts?"

"Well, Ohio."

"Oh, The Lawson Company."

"Yeah. You interested?"

"Yeah, tell me about it."

He told Frank that it had about 700 stores, a dairy, some real estate, and so on. Frank asked him if they had a "book" or prospectus on the Lawson chain giving details about it and Bucky said they did. Frank asked, "Why don't you send me the book?"

"Okay. Look, let's do that. If we don't make it, we don't make it. I understand, but if we don't have something to talk about, we're going to lose all the groundwork we've done and getting to know each other."

Everyone in the convenience store business knew that The Lawson Company was a pioneer in the field. J.C. Lawson started his first store back in the 1940s and invented the gallon jug of milk.

J.C. sold out to Consolidated Food around 1960 and 25 years later that became Sara Lee, a $9 billion company of which Lawson was only a tiny three percent and becoming a burden to run.

Frank, who was Vice President of Corporate Development at

the time, came into my office and told me about his conversation with Bucky. I suppose if I had been in my right mind again I would have said, "Are you crazy or something? Get out of here."

But I was always open to the Chain Belt of Opportunity, and here it was coming along that Belt again being presented to us.

So I said, "Well, that depends on the price and if we can make a profitable chain out of it."

And, I went on to say, "They were once a fine company, but today everybody in the business looks at them as a neglected operation that's run down. Call Bucky back and tell him we'd like to look at it."

Charlie never thought things were impossible. He would always tell people, "We can do it." So, things just happened.

I think that, over the years, as Charlie develops faith in people, and, as he develops trust, those people get more and more latitude. And, so, over the years it's a mutual understanding. "Look, you do your job and you're fine." If you don't, then you've got to contend with Charlie. That's the deal. And, everybody knew it. However, I don't remember Charlie ever being unfair.

—Frank Colaccino, CEO, Dairy Mart

It was May of 1985. Frank and Larry Handler and I went to Cuyahoga Falls, Ohio, to Lawson's headquarters to meet Lawson's President, Frank Alger, whom I had known when he was executive vice-president of Cumberland Farms, a large New England competitor.

We looked at about a dozen stores. They had potential, but many of them were low volume. Next, we dug into their books and saw they had 692 stores, a dairy plant to supply them, and some wholesale supermarket accounts and that they owned about 20 percent of the real estate their stores were on. This last part made the deal look sweeter than before, because you always like to own the real estate and we only owned about 10 percent of ours. At the same time, many of their stores were low volume operations, and that wasn't good.

I had seen and heard enough to know I wanted to go for it if it were possible. Here we were a company with a net worth of

$7 million and we were looking at a company with a net worth of $32 million, but believed that we would have to pay around $50 million to get it. We thought there was substantial value that wasn't even on the books. We left Cuyahoga Falls impressed. On the return flight, I smiled and thought, "I have just seen the perfect example of *The Chain Belt of Opportunity*."

The Belt was still to the left of me, not quite to the center yet, so I still had time to make up my mind before it got to the center. But by the time the plane landed, I had pretty much made up my mind and told Frank to call Bucky and tell him we needed to talk to him.

Then we got into discussions with the people at Shearson Lehman about the details of a possible deal. We did not yet know what the Lawson Stores would eventually go for, but knew there would be other bidders. Still, we went to our meeting with Shearson Lehman in New York with high hopes. I had to talk because The Chain Belt was still moving.

Bucky brought some other people into the meeting. One was Betty Eveillard, who was in charge of the sale for Sara Lee at Shearson. The other was Marc Bergschneider, whom Shearson had assigned to look after our interests if a deal came about. This was their way of avoiding a conflict of interest and being fair to both parties.

After some preliminary talk, we worked our way down to price. It was time for us to throw a figure on the table.

We decided to use our normal figure of $100,000 per store as the basis for our offer to Lawson. Some companies had been paying anywhere from $200,000 to $300,000, but I knew that was too much. That was proven in years to come when some of those companies went belly up. We also assumed that we might close as many as 200 of those 692 stores because they didn't pay.

So in our thought process, our opening base price was $40 million for the stores, but the 125 stores with owned real estate, the milk plant, and the home office had to be worth another $20 million. So our possible price became $60 million, but, obviously, we didn't start bidding at that figure.

Sara Lee wanted to sell, so that was in our favor. Also, there weren't many legitimate buyers around even though there were always the nitpickers and lookers and shoppers. We knew the convenience store business and we were serious, and we thought that would also be in our favor.

So this is how we arrived at our opening offer of $40 million, which of course, we didn't have, nor did we expect to buy at that price. Larry, Frank, and I laid it on the table in a private meeting with Marc Bergschneider, who was representing us at Shearson Lehman. We asked him how we were going to get the money.

Marc's solution was simple, "We'll sell some more stock. I think we can sell a $35 million debenture offering. If we sell another million shares of stock at $10 a share, that will give you $45 million. The stock might go as high as $14 or $15 a share. Either way, you'll have the money you need to buy the Lawson stores."

Then, Marc suggested we would need to up our bid. We increased our offer to $45 million and sat back impatiently to wait for the whale to get organized and give the guppy an answer. Meantime, we had to work out another problem.

There would be a gap between our signing a deal and having the money to pay for it. To go to a stock offering, we had to dance the dance of the SEC and they don't jitterbug, they waltz —slowly. So we needed some money in between closing the deal and getting the proceeds of the new stock and debenture sale. We needed what is called in the financial trade "bridge financing."

Our first resource for bridge financing should have been our bank, the Bank of Boston, so we went to talk with the bankers there.

I recall very well the meeting we had in Boston with those bankers who were led by a particular senior vice president. I knew the minute I was introduced to him that we were in deep trouble. He was an ultraconservative, old-line banker without vision, but with a Boston Brahmin name followed by three sticks. He couldn't possibly conceive of a 200-store company with a net worth of $7 million buying a 700-store company and bridging $45 million.

Marc Bergschneider presented our case, but the senior banker asked that Shearson Lehman guarantee repayment. Marc, of course, could not make that guarantee, but said that Shearson Lehman was prepared to give a "highly confident" letter. The senior banker didn't say "no" and he didn't say "yes," but I knew he meant "no."

It was a bitter setback for me, in a lifetime that had an ample share of setbacks. Fortunately for me, the management team I'd picked years earlier could be counted on when it was fourth down and nine. Larry Handler had already started looking for other sources of bridge financing.

Pat Lajudice, a vice president at The Connecticut Bank and Trust Company, had been soliciting Larry for our business, so Larry told him of our problem.

Pat got excited about the possibility of doing our bridge financing and getting our business so he went to work trying to get the details sorted out. After a lot of meetings and negotiations, The Connecticut Bank and Trust Company finally agreed to put up $32 million as a bridge loan.

We were still $13 million short, but had an idea that might sound strange to some people and was just creative financing to us. We went to Sara Lee and asked them to guarantee the remaining $13 million. Anxious to make the deal, as we thought they would be, they agreed and we had the $45 million we needed.

This took us from June 7th, the day of the meeting at the Bank of Boston, to July 11th, when we flew to Chicago to sign the initial agreement with the Sara Lee people that outlined our deal with them. The final agreement was signed on September 10, 1985, with retroactive takeover dated to July 1st. In our business, the months of July and August are the most profitable. It was that retroactive takeover date included in our quarterly statement that helped the stock come out at a good price.

The stock issue came out on November 15th, so as it turned out, we only needed the bridge for a little over two months.

We, of course, did a presentation that Wall Street calls "a dog and pony show" with the underwriters. I spent most of my time going to prospective investors in New York, Chicago, Los Angeles, in fact all over the country, to sell our stock. As I spoke to the various groups, I felt I was being received with enthusiasm, but when the stock finally came out, I was truly amazed when it opened at $22 a share instead of the $10 a share we had originally anticipated. The public obviously had a great deal more faith in the guppy than the Bank of Boston!

> *The Lawson deal was extraordinary. What it meant for Charlie . . . he understood what it was to take over a larger company . . . it didn't go to his head. Obviously, he was delighted by it and he loved the attention he got for doing an extraordinary difficult deal.*
> —Ford Goldman

Dairy Mart now had $22 million for the stock issue and the $35 million debenture, for a total of $57 million. We bought the Lawson stores for $45 million and had $12 million in reserve for the next time *The Chain Belt of Opportunity* started to move again!

But that $12 million did not sit in the bank long, because that money was burning a hole in my pocket and I had my eye on the chain belt. Growth is what I had always wanted, and we were getting very close to that ultimate goal of 1,000 stores.

However, an unexpected problem came to the surface soon after the guppy swallowed the whale.

CHAPTER XXXIV

Threats From the Inside

WE SIGNED OUR agreement to buy Lawson Stores on September 10th, and our 200-store chain became a 900-store chain. Frank Alger, the president of Lawson, said to me, "You know, Charlie, you were a small company last week and now you are a large company. A really big company. We operate differently in a big company."

I just smiled at the time, but on September 15th I was introduced and spoke to 350 Lawson Store managers at a trade show and told them, "You know, just last week Dairy Mart was a 200-store company. It was a small company. But as we gather today, Dairy Mart is a 900-store company. And I want to tell you something and I want to tell it to you straight. We are still a small company and we will continue to be and act like a small company."

The next day I said the same thing to a second group of 350 Lawson managers.

I don't know what Frank Alger thought about my statement, but he probably thought I was some kind of nut who didn't know how to run a big business. However, because of what he said to me that day, I really did go to work and try to make the 900 store company a small company. A company with the personal touch. And I have to tell you that we succeeded.

At one point, Frank Alger wasn't sure he would fit in and, after one of our meetings, had offered to resign when Dairy Mart took over, but I convinced him not to.

But there are often some problems in running a company, large or small, and some of our new problems that came with the acquisition of Lawson Stores surfaced before long.

One was with a labor union, the International Brotherhood of Teamsters, Chauffeurs, Warehousemen and Helpers of America, Local 336, to which our dairy plant employees belonged, and it was basically about money and power. The Teamsters Union had a contract with The Lawson Company that expired on December 15th. The apparent issue was money, but I suspect the real issue was power. The Teamsters wanted to stake out their turf with the new management immediately so we would have no illusions as to who was in charge.

The money issue was that Lawson's plant workers in Ohio were getting over 25% more an hour, including benefits, than our Connecticut workers were getting for doing exactly the same thing. The Teamsters told us they wanted even more or they would strike.

We said we were paying too much as it was, but were willing to continue paying at that level. However, we wouldn't pay more than that. Then, the union did a stupid thing. They struck our plant. So, the union didn't understand its opponent and made the wrong move. More than once.

First it was a picket line, but after the first of the year, we had to get the plant back in operation and hire replacement workers. When the union pickets got over the shock of that, they turned vicious. Other dairies in the area were helping keep our stores supplied, but we soon had our plant back running.

Another mistake the union leadership made was to strike at a time when there was nine percent unemployment in the area. We had no trouble finding 125 workers to replace the 150 union workers at 25% less per hour than was being demanded by the union.

Then things got serious. First it was slingshots and lead pellets through our windows at about ten stores every night. After that, union members threatened the replacement workers, tried to attack them, spat on them, and beat on the cars and trucks coming in and out of the plant.

Finally, a security guard was shot at the plant. We had no proof as to who was doing this, but we had never had these kind of problems before.

Then came the worst blow of all when the phone rang at the office on April 1 while I was there.

"We have just poisoned the milk at seven of your stores."

The caller hung up.

The first thing that hit me was, what kind of people, what kind of monsters, would poison innocent people? The second thing that hit me was, who would come to the stores to buy milk anyway once the story got out? So we immediately ordered all the milk out of our 700 stores.

The milk was hauled back to the plant, where we had independent chemists test every batch, only to find that none of it had been poisoned. Naturally, the press—more interested in sensationalism—headlined the scare with "LAWSON MILK POISONED!" A later edition story reporting that independent chemists' tests showed the milk safe was buried in the back pages.

We had a serious problem. We were without milk in our stores for a week, and even when we put it back in, sales were understandably slow.

This was a tough go for us and we were at a disadvantage, being new management and in places like Cleveland and Akron, which are strong labor towns. Still, we have never regretted standing up to the union. We listened to them, tried to reason with them, but we'll be damned if they can take over our company and run it.

It is now seven years since the unions in Ohio walked out of our plant and they have never been back in.

What has happened since then is that we repainted and refurbished the Lawson stores and converted them into Dairy Marts. Modern equipment replaced the older stuff, shelf space increased, and new items and novelty ice cream cases were installed. The result has been increased volume, happier employees, and increased profits.

Lawson was run by Frank Alger, as I said, and his style was

bureaucratic, in that he didn't mix with his people, but kept himself insulated behind a barrier of eight vice presidents.

That's not my style. Our operation was and is quite different, because we don't have "report-tos" as much as we *"work with"* people. We "work with" all the people, and "we" included me. We're more like coaches who listen to the people we "work with." It's really not management versus labor. It's an "us" organization, not an us-against-them organization.

So, there was a great difference between Alger's style at Lawson and mine at Dairy Mart, but we were in a bind during the summer of 1985 while we were still negotiating to buy Lawson. We hadn't made a final deal and the Sara Lee people made it clear that they wouldn't sell if we didn't have the support of Frank Alger and his management team of eight vice-presidents whom he called "reports."

I invited Frank and his wife to my Cape Cod home over the Fourth of July. I wanted to talk with him away from day-to-day business activities .

Frank and I took a walk along the beach that weekend to discuss the pending deal.

"I'll tell you what we're going to do. Dairy Mart will give you stock options for 100,000 shares. Right now, it's selling for $10, but I have a hunch it's going to sell for considerably more once this deal is closed. But we will guarantee it to you at the $10 price to divide between you and your key people."

He didn't say anything at the moment, so I went on to complete my thought.

"I think you should have 40,000 of those shares and the other 60,000 should go to your vice-presidents. What do you think?"

"Let me think about that."

The next day we were out walking on the beach again.

"You know, I like your idea of giving us 100,000 shares, but I think I should get 60,000 and the others should divide the 40,000."

It shocked me at the time, but it also told me a lot about Frank.

"I think we ought to be a little fairer than that. Remember, there are eight of them and only one of you. But we realize you're the key man. So what would you think about your taking 50,000 shares and dividing the other 50,000 with the eight others?"

He hesitated and, sensing that his earlier greed had been a mistake, agreed to this arrangement. Then I decided to get him even more solidly on our side, "You know, you're a great guy and you have a lot of talent. I'm getting older and I would like to see you become president of the entire Dairy Mart company. Take over all 900 stores so I can take it a little easier."

He liked that. He liked that a lot, and I had been looking for a president for the company. I had four top executives who all wanted to be president, but they were still relatively young. Naming Frank Alger president when he was 58 would solve the problem for me and still keep the other four interested in succeeding him in a few more years.

Frank and I agreed he would become president of Dairy Mart on January 1st, 1986, soon after we closed the Lawson deal. It turned out that I hadn't solved a problem. I had created one.

CHAPTER XXXV

The Self-Appointed, Self-Anointed

ONE TYPE OF person I have never had much patience with is the self-appointed, self-anointed savior who knows how everybody else must live their lives.

Others have noted that these people, like Jimmy Swaggart and Jim and Tammy Bakker, have an Elmer Gantry arrogance that is hard for most people to take. But, hey, I'm in the convenience store business and busy serving the needs of my customers. What do I have to do with people like that anyhow? Unfortunately, a whole lot more than I wish I did.

Down in Tupelo, Mississippi, there was this Reverend Donald Wildmon whom nobody ever heard of until he formed his National Federation of Decency, which was dedicated to telling everyone else how to live. It has since changed its name to the American Family Association, but it is still the same leopard with the same spots.

In 1986, Wildmon decided his group had nothing better to do than attack convenience stores that sold what his group had decided were pornographic magazines, specifically, *Playboy* and *Penthouse*. These people threatened the biggest convenience store chain in the country, Southland's 7-Eleven, with a boycott until these magazines were banned from their stores.

Unfortunately, Southland, with its roots in conservative, evangelical Dallas, caved in and did as Wildmon demanded.

Bloated with that easy victory, Wildmon thought other convenience chains would be as easy to pick off as stragglers in a cattle herd. He found out differently when he tangled with us.

He started by attacking our Lawson stores and rallying support for banning the magazines HE had decided were unacceptable for grownups to read. These, of course, were magazines dealing with adult sexual matters, but nothing was said about magazines dealing with violence, mayhem, or killing. Those, presumably, were all right for people to read. And, of course, next on the list could be magazines promoting political views with which the good Reverend disagreed. I could see him demanding that only "politically correct" magazines be sold and magazines that didn't conform with his religious calling be banned.

Of course, he was so busy raising big money in the same way Swaggart and the Bakkers did, I didn't see how he had time to read these magazines he was upset about. This was the scare niche he had picked out for his previously obscure church, and he said that I was to stop selling these magazines.

Well, I couldn't bring myself to tell adults what they should and shouldn't read. We already had these magazines behind the counter, where the cashier enforced a strict policy of selling to adults only and insisted on identification when necessary. We had them in special individual racks where no one could even see the covers and minors couldn't thumb through them.

But Mr. Wildmon appeared to want to dictate what magazines are moral and, hence, what magazines would be available to the nation's adult readers. I had read too much, probably in politically incorrect magazines that Mr. Wildmon would have banned if he could, about this kind of stuff taking place in Nazi Germany. I wondered why some people think they're so smart they should decide what other people shall or shall not read?

Because I refused to obey his dictates, Wildmon mounted a boycott of our Lawson stores about three months after the strike began. So now we had both the teamsters and the League of Decency picketing us. I knew how to handle the union, but I admit I had a difficult time deciding how to handle Wildmon's League.

The boycott was hurting our stores, but I and my buddies fought in a war to preserve the freedom of speech and freedom of press that this guy was trying to bring down. Still, I didn't want to be bullheaded. I didn't want to act hastily.

The answer came one night, and Jan was the first to know about it because, poor thing, I was so excited about the idea I woke her out of a sound sleep to explain it to her. I decided to let my customers vote. I would use the American way to answer the question. If the majority wanted the magazines out of the stores, out they would go.

The election took place in all of our Ohio stores for three weeks, starting May 20th, and we recorded 456,000 ballots cast. To be fair, we got Ohio's former attorney general to supervise the counting of the ballots.

Of course, this gave Mr. Wildmon a fit, because he didn't care about what the majority wanted, but we did. Then, he counterattacked and it demonstrated what kind of American he was. He rented buses and filled them with his supporters and shuttled them from store to store day after day all day long to vote and essentially stuff the ballot boxes. And, of course, these people weren't our regular customers anyhow. In fact, they jammed up our places so much that it drove many of our regular customers away, at tremendous cost to us.

The result was predictable. Most Americans immediately get their backs up when people try to tell them how to think or act. In spite of Mr. Wildmon's ballot stuffing tactics, he could only put together 35 percent of the vote.

"My customers have spoken. They wanted the right to decide for themselves what they will read. The magazines will stay."

Wildmon and his narrow group screamed to the high heavens and said that they would continue to boycott our stores no matter what.

However, Reverend Wildmon was not the only one who wanted to tell the people what they can read. I am going to close this chapter with an exchange of correspondence that speaks for itself:

City of Ravenna
[City Seal]

April 1, 1988

Mr. Charles Nirenberg, Chairman
Dairy Mart, Inc.

Dear Mr. Nirenberg,

On behalf of the City of Ravenna, I would like to welcome Dairy Mart to the Ravenna Community.

I like your slogan, "the good people" store. I know that the people who are employed in the local Dairy Mart are good people. This is evident by the noticeable cleanliness of the stores both inside and out. Also, the courteousness extended to each customer is appreciated . . .

However, there is one area of the Dairy Mart business that troubles me. That is the sale of pornographic magazines. Quite frankly, I am surprised that Dairy Mart chooses to sell pornography, being a "good people" business . . .

As Mayor and Safety Director for the City of Ravenna, I am concerned for the safety, health, and welfare of the Ravenna citizens and their families. After extensive personal research on the effects [physical and emotional] that obscene materials have on individuals, [I believe] without any doubt in my mind, that obscene material, which includes pornography, does not promote the safety, health, and welfare of the Ravenna citizen. In fact, pornography promotes just the opposite; the improper and perverted view of human sexuality—which has an immoral, debilitating, and destructive effect on individuals and their families. God designed human sexuality to be good and wholesome between husband and wife only. Sexual intimacy in a marriage is just one of the many beautiful ways of expressing the love the married couple have for each other. Pornography transforms human sexuality from love to lust . . .

Sincerely,

Donald J. Kainrad, Mayor

DAIRY MART
[logo]

April 8, 1988

Dear Mayor Kainrad,

I appreciate the time you took to write me about the "good people" of Dairy Mart and our stores in Portage County, Ohio. We work hard to make them clean, neat, full and friendly, and it's great to know people like you value our efforts.

Clearly, too, you have also voiced concerns about our stores' selling adult-oriented magazines . . . Assume for an instant that the reasons you so eloquently state for not selling adult magazines are heeded and acted upon by every possible outlet for these magazines. Where do we draw the line? Where do we stop dictating values? Shouldn't cigarettes be removed from sale to avoid societal harm, or alcohol, or even milk [high cholesterol], for that matter?

If we remove ourselves from the rights of choice, then any governmental body or a committee of a select few can dictate what we read, eat, wear, or do for a living. I don't think you are a proponent of that form of government.

It was in this spirit of democracy, free speech, and the American way that we put the issues you brought up to a vote . . . to anyone who came to our stores, to our customers. In a well-publicized and certified election, people entering our stores all over Ohio were given the right to vote adult magazines in or out. Overwhelmingly, the vote indicated that the customers want the right to choose whether or not they buy adult magazines.

Mayor Kainrad, I am not trying to be combative with you; nor am I willing to engage in a running discourse on the subject. But I do respect your position. I hope you respect the position of all American consumers, of their right to decide for themselves what they want to purchase.

Very truly yours,
Charles Nirenberg
Chairman of the Board and
Chief Executive Officer
DAIRY MART CONVENIENCE
STORES, INC.

CHAPTER XXXVI

Reaching the Magic Number

I INSTALLED FRANK Alger as the President of Dairy Mart at the beginning of January, 1986. His management style was much different from mine. His was much more bureaucratic, but I hoped he would succeed. I truly wanted him to succeed, but couldn't help wondering how my people would adjust to his management style.

The combination of his experience and our family style of operation should have blended to produce an effective method of operation.

I remember well one of the first speeches I made to the Lawson employees where I broke down the components of the word FAMILY.

"F is for family and every family needs a father image and that's me. I look old enough to be a father to most of you, so just think of me as the Colonel Sanders of Dairy Mart.

"A is for attitude and the most important thing is an attitude of respect for oneself and one's company.

"M is for motivation and I want people working who *want to* do things—*want to* go places—because this company is going places. And, I want you to go and grow with us.

"I is for the individual. To me, you're a name, a person, not just store 5199. You're not a number and we're not going to treat you like a number.

"L is for listening. You've got to *listen* to your employees. *Listen* to your customers. *Listen* to your suppliers. Listen to your managers. Because, when you listen, you learn.

"Y, finally, is for yes as in yes, we can do it. Get a positive attitude. It can work miracles for you and for Dairy Mart.

"This is what family is all about and this is what your company is all about. Together we are a family!"

After Frank was installed as the new President, I took my usual vacation in Jamaica. Normally when I'm in Jamaica, I call the office once a week, but something made me call several times a week. It didn't take long for me to realize that things were not going well. So I told Jan that I felt I should go back to Enfield for about a week and asked her if she minded being alone. She said it was no problem. I returned and talked with my key people and quickly decided to fly to Cuyahoga Falls for a meeting with Frank Alger.

"Well, how do you think things are going?"

"I don't think they're going too good."

"I think you're right. I don't think they're going too good either."

He said nothing.

"What do you think we ought to do?"

"I don't know. What do you think we should do?"

"Well, Frank, you offered your resignation once before right after you were installed as President. Perhaps I should have accepted it because I don't see things getting better."

He stared off into space, pondering our brief conversation, which had long range implications for both of us. Then, reluctantly, "I guess you're right. It doesn't look like it's going to work out."

We agreed Frank would leave Dairy Mart April 1st. Luckily, Steve Montgomery was already in Ohio understudying Alger's job in running the Lawson operation. I had sent Steve to Ohio to learn about the Lawson stores. With 700 stores involved, I had to have someone ready to step in and run the Lawson Stores when Frank moved to Enfield or just in case something happened to Frank. Well, something had happened to Frank and we were ready.

The transition went fairly smoothly, and on April 1st, Steve became President of the Lawson Division and Frank's time with Dairy Mart was over. Without Frank, the operation changed dramatically.

Steve had to turn Alger's eight "report-to" vice-presidents into "work with" vice-presidents. We hoped most would stay with Dairy Mart, but frankly we didn't need them all. Lawson's was a mini-Giant Stores in that it had too many people in administration.

One of the vice-presidents resigned along with Frank. Most of the others had their little empires, which wouldn't be tolerated in Dairy Mart, and they ultimately left. We now have two of the eight, and they fit into our team system.

Alger made out fine. When he left, we paid him six months severance, and Sara Lee also gave him six months. He immediately joined Cumberland Farms Stores as a consultant, and he ended up making a very handsome mid-six-figure profit with the Dairy Mart stock options given to him. Not bad for six months with the company.

With the Lawson deal behind us and things settling down it was getting too quiet for me and I started thinking again about my magic goal of 1,000 stores. We still had that extra $12 million we had taken in from the new stock offering.

These thoughts naturally turned me to my friend Joe Peden. He was in the convenience store business as the CEO of the CONNA Corporation, based in Louisville, Kentucky. CONNA operated 369 stores and was the main regional franchisee for Convenient Food Mart based in Chicago.

Joe was having trouble with Convenient Food Mart. Convenient Food Mart had initiated an unfriendly takeover of CONNA and weren't willing to pay more than $10 a share for CONNA. It was a strange situation. CONNA's main asset was the Convenient Food Mart franchises and CONNA couldn't transfer the franchises without permission of the Convenient Food Mart. It would seem that Joe Peden and CONNA were over a barrel.

Convenient Food Mart was headed by Dick Fisher and Stanley Bressler, both of whom were known to be difficult and crude. Some thought Fisher and Bressler enjoyed hurting people.

Joe Peden was just the opposite—a true, soft-spoken Southern Gentleman who had been a leader in the convenience store industry. One day I called Joe to commiserate with him and see if I could help him or if there might be an opportunity for Dairy Mart. Joe knew I wasn't calling to say hello or to check the weather in Louisville.

"Well, Charlie, I really don't know what we can do. Do you?"

"First off, Joe, your company is worth a lot more than $10 a share, so why don't I come in as a *white knight*? I'd like to look your company over, but right off the top of my head I would say it's worth more like $20 a share."

Joe knew he would probably end up being forced to sell, but he would rather sell to a friend who would pay him a decent price than to the Chicago boys. The following week, I came to Louisville and made a presentation to CONNA's Board of Directors. They liked what I said and it became a friendly takeover effort.

Once again, many people would ask if I had lost my mind still another time, and the answer again would probably be "Yes." To someone else, it would be stupid to buy a company when I would have to get permission of a hostile franchisor who wanted the company itself.

I went to Chicago and met with Fisher and Bressler. As I usually did, I just laid the deal on the table. I told them Dairy Mart had just signed a tentative deal with CONNA, subject to Convenient Food Mart's approval, and we were ready to become a franchisee of theirs.

Fisher and Bressler were fit to be tied. They ranted and raved.

"You guys would be smart if you just picked up your deal and walked away because we're not letting you in. Don't waste your time on this one."

That, of course, pushed one of my most famous hot buttons. They didn't know Charlie Nirenberg, because when someone tells me I can't do something, it simply becomes a challenge to get it done. When I walked into their office, I thought this would be a nice deal to make. Now it had been changed into a must-do deal.

"It's too bad you feel that way. We're going ahead with the deal and I'm not walking away."

That took them aback and they regrouped, with the result that we agreed to meet again in two weeks in New York at the office of their attorney, Natalie Koether, along with Ford Goldman.

The meeting didn't start well with Fisher blustering loudly, "Look, I'm going to tell you something and I'm going to tell it to you straight. If you were smart, you'd back away from this deal. Just get out now. I don't think you should bid. Just pick up and walk away. I have more money than you and you're never going to get these stores."

I tried the quiet approach. "You know, Dick, it is great that you have more money than me, but you've got to remember that means you have more money to lose than I have."

That brought him back to earth. This was the second time he had tried to scare me and it hadn't worked, so we talked some more and decided on a third meeting in Chicago.

This time I had Larry Handler and Ford Goldman with me, and after some preliminaries, Fisher made an offer.

"I'll tell you what we'll do. We'll take half the stores and you can have half. We'll just split them down the middle. How's that sound to you, Charlie?"

It sounded to me like they were backing off from a fight because they knew that, even if they won, they would get blooded. In some ways it was like that fist fight I had with Mike Cassidy when I was a kid. I might get beaten, but the other guy would get hurt, too.

Fisher's proposal brought a smile to my face, because I realized I had finally gotten through to these two.

"You know, Dick, I've got to tell you, this reminds me of the story of Solomon. When two women came before him and both of them were claiming a little baby was theirs and Solomon the Wise had to decide which one was the real mother. So he said, 'Let's cut the baby in half and you can both have a half.' And one of the women said, 'No, no. Let her have the baby.' So Solomon gave the baby to this woman because she would rather give the baby up than have it cut in half. He knew that the real mother would react this way. We're not going to cut this baby in half either, Dick. I want all of the stores."

We talked and talked. I realized I had to give Dick and Stan something. So, a few days later, while I was vacationing at my Cape Cod home, I received a call from Dick and we agreed they would get 77 stores and we would get 292. The 77 were in Illinois, an area we did not cover—an area that was too distant for us—and in Massachusetts, where we may have had a conflict of interest. We paid $20 million for all the stores and sold the 77 to the Convenient Food Marts for $5 million, and we paid for it with the $12 million we had in the bank and only borrowed $3 million.

It was now October of 1986, and the CONNA deal plus a few smaller ones gave us over 1,200 stores, of which about 450 sold gas.

The CONNA stores were profitable from day one, because they put us in the gasoline business and boosted us from a company selling 50 million gallons a year to one selling 200 million gallons of gas annually.

Finally, I had achieved my goal of 1,000 stores and then some. Now came another challenge: making sure what I had built would survive.

CHAPTER XXXVII

Fine-Tuning the Team

IN ONE WAY, we had gone a long ways in the last few years, but, by 1987, we were also like a slightly disorganized jail break. We needed tightening, honing, re-organizing and trimming.

What we actually had was three companies with three separate headquarters: Dairy Mart in Enfield, Connecticut; Lawson in Cuyahoga Falls, Ohio; and CONNA in Louisville, Kentucky. The three needed to be melded into one.

Steve Montgomery was running Lawson, and we lost money the first year because of both the union strike and the League of Decency boycott. Over all, our accountants and lawyers decided we had to set aside $3.3 million to cover all the claims that might come against pension fund reserves.

The League of Decency boycott continued to have some effect, but I wasn't going to give in on that one either. Plus, we had spent $6 million redoing all the Lawson stores and changing them to the kind of quality operation Dairy Mart was known for having. We dumped the Lawson name, because we discovered it had developed a bad image over the years and had become more of a liability than an asset.

The CONNA operation was hectic and bloated because initially, we had to carry more executives on the payroll than we really needed. For example, they hadn't let anybody go since we took over, but they were managing 77 fewer stores. Joe Peden was still there as Chairman, Bob Johnson as President, and Doug Vetter as Executive Vice President. Too top heavy.

So, in October, 1987, I had dinner with Joe and Bob along with Mitch Kupperman, my human resources expert. You should understand that, at this point, Joe Peden was Chairman of a company that didn't need a Chairman, but I allowed Joe to stay on for the better part of three years because it was the gentlemanly thing to do. Still, I wanted to deal with the other two top executives at dinner. "We have come down here to make some changes, Joe."

I explained that Bob, a highly regarded and knowledgeable administrator, had announced he would retire the following spring, and I didn't want Doug to think he would replace him. We'd tried to groom Doug in the Dairy Mart philosophy, but he never bought into it, and, besides, I had a strong sense that I had never had his loyalty. I just couldn't depend on him.

"Gentlemen, tomorrow morning when Doug arrives at the office, I am going to relieve him of his duties."

"What are you going to do?"

"Who are you going to hire?"

All I said was, "We'll think of something."

Of course, I had already decided to bring Frank Colaccino in to replace Doug. Frank was one of my four-member management team, along with Steve Montgomery, Larry Handler, and Mitch Kupperman.

We sent Frank Colaccino to the CONNA company and we didn't want to send Frank alone—he needed some support and we didn't know what kind of finance people they had there and they had no human resource department. So what we did was we sent Frank with the support of Greg Landry as his chief financial officer there and a human resource person that we took from the Midwest, Pat Cascarelli. The three of them went out there as a team.

The first month, Frank let 40 people go and started cutting off stores that weren't paying their way. This was tough, but necessary if you care about profits and survival in business. By the end of 1988, CONNA showed a substantial increase in profits.

Greg was a great help. He had first come to Dairy Mart

company about the time we were expanding fast. It was when we made the Lawson acquisition and, soon beyond that, the CONNA acquisition. He started out as the number three man in the finance department and we didn't really see Greg come into his own until 1987 at the time when we sent Frank Colaccino out to CONNA and when we fired Doug Vetter.

That's when Greg began to shine as chief financial officer of a division and that's when he started to learn how to work with Frank Colaccino. Frank did what I normally did with people, that is, train them, teach them, let them know what was expected from them.

He and Frank ended up making an excellent team out of the CONNA corporation when they did such a wonderful job of bringing them into a profitable position. Frank, of course, was the leader and he was running that division. Greg was his right-hand man and he did an excellent job.

Now, I think it has to be mentioned that under adverse circumstances he did an excellent job. They lost their entire finance department. They lost their entire computer department. Doug Vetter went out and started a company for Convenient Food Mart right in Louisville, Kentucky. Most of CONNA's computer people left with Doug. Here we were the most important franchisee of Convenient Food Mart and they were apparently enticing our computer people to depart.

Greg ended up losing most of his people and still shining—re-hiring new people—one of whom was Jeff Jones who has since then become the Treasurer of the company and is the number two man to Greg Landry at this time.

Greg has since proven himself to be an excellent chief financial officer for the total company in many ways. Not only in fine record keeping and in being a leader in the finance department, but, more particularly, in his relationships with banks and institutions. That's where a chief financial officer makes a real difference to a company because the kind of relationship you have with your banks and financial institutions makes the difference as to whether you can get the money or cannot get the money to expand the company. That's Greg's forte and I think he's done a terrific job.

Speaking of computers, that was my first big step to consolidating the three operations. Not only was each one headquartered in a different place geographically, each one had a different computer system, and none of them could talk with one another. So in 1987 we started to install a new, coordinated system. They say that computers can do your work faster, but it wasn't until 1990 that the installation of the new system was complete.

CHAPTER XXXVIII

Trying a Leveraged Buy-Out

AFTER THINGS STARTED pulling together in business, I reached a landmark in my personal life.

I turned 65 on December 13, 1988. It is one of those milestone birthdays that make you think about your life and where it's going. I suppose our 21st, 40th and 50th birthdays are those kinds of milestones and I know for sure my 65th was. It made me think about putting my estate in order and looking to the future.

I had a good team in place with Frank, Steve, Larry and Mitch so I could look to the future with confidence, but I wouldn't be around forever and wanted to prepare for that day.

One of the things that was attractive was a Leveraged Buy Out [LBO] which was the wave of business in the 1980s. This was a financial mechanism whereby a buyer used the assets of a company to borrow the money necessary to buy the controlling stock of the company. In effect, the company financed the purchase of itself. Or, there was always the possibility that I could have sold control of the company outright to an outside buyer.

I have my own philosophy of what to do when faced with decisions of this type. You never take a one-way street and expect to stay on it. I always like to go down the street until I come to a Y. Then, I make up my mind which road to take. And, even when I go that way, I don't rule out finding yet another Y in the road.

So, I had explored both arms of the Y. I talked over the possibility of an LBO with Salomon Brothers and I talked with the Getty Oil people about selling to them.

The Getty arm of the Y seemed smoother and I gravitated toward it. Leo Lebowitz, the President of Getty, liked to move fast, the way I did, and we had the basics of a deal put together by the time I came back from my Jamaica vacation in April, 1989. We shook hands on it and put the attorneys and accountants to work.

Getty knew the gas business and wanted to get into convenience stores because the marriage of these industries was inevitable. Dairy Mart had become the shining star of convenience stores. We were growing and making money, and we had already gotten our feet more than wet in the gasoline business. Getty was big, but not too big. We were big, but not too big. They needed a lot of what we had and we needed a lot of what they had. It looked like the perfect merger.

Then, Salomon Brothers heard about my deal with Getty and asked for a meeting.

"Why are you doing this deal with Getty? We can give you everything Getty is giving you and you can still own the company."

That was a statement that got my attention. They were going to give me the price per share Getty was going to pay and keep me on for five years. I took Ford Goldman into the other room.

"Ford, is this for real? Can they really do this? I mean they're giving me what Getty's giving. Can they do everything they say they're going to do?"

"Yes, Charlie. Salomon Brothers has done its homework."

"But, what are the chances this can succeed? Is it for real? Can it fail?"

"If Salomon Brothers says they are going to do the deal, they are prepared to do the deal. These people know what they're doing. They don't play games. They wouldn't have come all the way to Hartford if they felt there was only a remote chance it would succeed."

If I thought there was only a 90% chance Salomon would do the deal, I wouldn't have taken it. As it was, I said, "Let's go."

Later, at a meeting with my top people, I told them what Ford had said and that I felt they would be in a stronger position with the LBO than with the Getty deal. I would still be in charge and my key team would still be there. Management would have 62 1/2 percent of the company and Salomon would have 37 1/2 percent of the company. I would always be in control and everyone would be protected from any changes after the deal was finalized. That probably wouldn't be the case if I went with the Getty deal. Everybody agreed the LBO was the way to go.

I could have waited until Salomon's deal was set, but that wouldn't have been fair to Leo, so I called him and leveled with him immediately. It wasn't an easy phone call.

"You know, Leo, we haven't signed a deal yet and I am truly sorry to tell you, but we're calling the deal off."

"What's the matter, Charlie?"

"Well, after thinking about it, I think I can do the same thing you're offering me and come out better through an LBO."

"You're crazy. What if it doesn't work?"

"I've been told by people who know that it'll go."

"You're making a mistake, Charlie."

"Perhaps, but I have to call off our deal. I wanted you to know now, I don't want you to lose any money. You have sent people out here and have attorneys working and I don't want you to lose a penny. Please, Leo, bill us for their time."

He billed us for $30,000 and I sent him a check. I like to be fair with anyone I do business with. I like to make money the same as anyone, but it is not everything to me. Fairness, integrity and honesty mean a lot to me.

We signed our agreement with Salomon Brothers and announced that the management of Dairy Mart had formed a holding corporation called DMCS, Inc. [Dairy Mart Convenience Stores] and intended to buy *all* the stock—mine and that of all the other shareholders—of Dairy Mart at a premium price of $14.50 a share.

The Board hired Paine-Webber to give what is called "a fairness opinion," to opine, after a thorough evaluation, that the price was fair. After studying the situation for two months, they decided $15.00 a share was the fair price so we immediately upped our offer to that figure.

But the day we came out with the original $14.50 per share offer, a guy by the name of John Catsimatidis came in with a bid of $15.50 a share. Catsimatidis who headed United Refining Company, owned a group of convenience stores in Pennsylvania and his own refinery. Now we had competitive bids for Dairy Mart, but with regard to my personal Dairy Mart stock, I did not have to accept his bid or anyone else's bid. My wife and I owned a controlling position in the stock and we issued a public statement that we were selling our controlling stock only to DMCS.

Later, when we increased our offer from $14.50 to $15.00 a share to conform to Paine Webber's fairness opinion, Catsimatidis came out with an offer of $16.00 a share. So we restated our determination to sell our stock to no one but the management group. That put an end to the Catsimatidis bidding.

Meanwhile, the Salomon team of Mike Zimmerman, Peter Venetis, and Michael Klein were putting the deal together and had us meet with a number of banks in Boston and New York to seek the $80 million financing package that was necessary. We decided to go with the Bank of Boston. We liked the way Bank of Boston was the first one to respond and say that they were ready to do business with us. Others came along later, but Salomon liked the way Bank of Boston moved fast and with no nonsense or hesitation. So we decided to go with them and they sent us a letter of intent on May 20, 1989. They appeared committed and we had, we believed, the $80 million we needed lined up.

The total package necessary for the deal was $150 million. There was Dairy Mart's existing $35 million debentures which would stay in place and we also needed an additional $35 million of debentures. We would have to pay the stockholders in the neighborhood of $65 million and the rest was for the company's working capital and some expansion capital.

Everything looked good and we figured we were on easy street and the green light was on. We were only waiting for the SEC to finish its work on the papers we had submitted on June 15 and give us clearance which was expected about August 1.

Then, the Bank of Boston hit us with a staggering blow on

July 20th. The bank faxed Salomon Brothers a letter saying they were backing out of the deal. They used the flimsy excuse that Dairy Mart hadn't made budget in May and June. The Bank of Boston didn't even give us the courtesy of a letter or a telephone call.

To get some answers about what was going on, we went to Boston and sat down with the bankers for a talk. We explained exactly how we expected to make our budget and why we sincerely believed we could. But there was no way we could convince them. They were just putting on a show for us and acting like they were listening. Later, we figured out that banks were bailing out of LBOs all over the place. Had the Bank of Boston not balked, we probably would have completed the deal within a matter of weeks as scheduled.

The truth of the matter is that we not only made up for not making budget for those two months but ended the year by making more profit than the budget called for.

Unfortunately it didn't help. We didn't have the financing we needed. It would have been a good deal for the stockholders who would get $15 a share for their stock which, when readjusted for stock splits and stock dividends, essentially cost them around $2.70 a share if they had purchased the stock in the 1983 initial public offering. In other words, if the LBO would have gone through, all the shareholders would have been a lot happier and a lot richer.

However, I didn't give up that easy. We went back to Salomon to see what else we could do to bring off the LBO. They helped us and approached other financial institutions, but banks were having problems and cutting back on LBO deals. After a while, the sources were talking an interest rate of 18 percent and that would have killed us even if they had said yes. Plus those that were talking at all were talking only $10 a share for the stock.

Catsimatidis wasn't interested anymore at the $16 a share he had once been so anxious to offer. Of course, Getty Oil was no longer interested and I could hardly blame them.

The truth of the matter was that the economy was starting to tighten down and banks and businesses were in real trouble all over the nation.

On October 30, 1989 we pulled the LBO off the market and I turned my thinking to other things.

So, the LBO was dead. So was the Getty deal. I said to myself, "Charlie, old boy, I think you blew it this time."

I had been through worse times and survived and always found things worked out for the best. I had a hunch they would this time, too!

CHAPTER XXXIX

Baa, Baa Braxton

THE FUTURE IS ahead and the past is behind. That's obvious, but many refuse to accept it as a fact.

I have never allowed myself to look back for very long and that was true in the case of the collapsed LBO. You can do something about the future. You can't do one earthly thing to change the past.

So, I put the failed LBO behind me and moved ahead, which meant going on to Stop-N-Go. While dealing with Salomon and the banks, we knew a chain of 137 convenience stores in Ohio and Michigan called Stop-N-Go was for sale by the Sun Oil Company.

The chain would be a perfect addition to our Midwest Division that was starting to make a good profit, and I had a hunch we could buy Stop-N-Go right.

As a sign of how I kept things moving, we aborted the LBO on October 30, 1989 and made the deal to buy Stop-N-Go from Sun Oil eleven days later. However, knowing that the convenience store business is slow during the winter months, we delayed closing the deal until March of 1990. That way we got Stop-N-Go and didn't have the winter negative effect on our financial statement.

We figured we'd have to close 10 or 20 of the stores, but that was built into our bargain price of under $10 million plus inventory, besides which, this chain had 52 stores selling gasoline which is a big plus.

When I say we figured we'd have to close 10 or 20 of the stores, that is common in the convenience store industry. We are closing below performance stores regularly while looking for new locations.

Some convenience store chains today are not doing well because they are more concerned with store numbers than profits. However, I know that Dairy Mart would not be doing as well if we didn't close stores. A businessman can't keep a business open solely on the HOPE that a poor store will improve. You have to constantly and critically re-evaluate your own business if you want to success.

In many ways that was a lesson I had learned early selling eggs and chickens from the farm in Millis. You can't ever stop checking on how you are doing and adjusting your operations accordingly.

We look at the bottom line of each store each month and, if a store is not making money or doesn't have a good or temporary reason for not showing a profit, we start watching it carefully. In the end, we turn it around in a hurry or we close it.

> Our forte has been we've always bought stores cheap. Then, we've gone in and closed bad stores immediately while up-grading the others. We weren't interested in numbers, we were interested in quality and that came from Charlie. Charlie would say, if a store's no good—close it. Don't have an ego about having a lot of stores. We're here to make money.
>
> —Frank Colaccino

Of course, closing a store is always hard to do because people are involved and, yet, it's something we must do if we're going to stay in business. Whenever possible, we absorb those people into our operation.

The Stop-N-Go Stores have been good to us and they have been profitable from day one. Some of their key people blended right into our organization, in fact, their top man,

Dave Beckman, joined us as director of operations and we gave him a region of around 250 stores to handle.

Dave has since been made a Vice President and we think very highly of him.

It was both interesting and depressing to attend the January, 1990, executive conference of the National Association of Convenience Stores just after our LBO folded and we missed the Getty deal. The Association had hired a company to study the future of the industry and this study, the Braxton Report, said the industry was in bad shape and the future was dark.

It struck me as curious because here was an industry that had grown by leaps and bounds, had been the darling of Wall Street, and now somebody was saying it was in trouble. Moreover, the report said the slump would last until 1995 and, then, the industry would begin to recover.

The report said the expansion potential of the 80,000 store industry was only 1,000 more stores in the next five years. This was a shock and everyone left the meeting shaking their heads in disbelief. It was particularly stunning to some of the smaller chains and to those that found business turning bad already.

I felt sorry for some of them, but walked away asking myself what I could do to make this Braxton Report work to my advantage. I knew I wasn't going to let it destroy me emotionally.

Some chains—big chains—such as 7-Eleven, Circle K and those two Chicago charmers at Convenient Food Marts were in severe financial difficulty and would all be in Chapter 11 bankruptcy before the year was out.

In contrast the industry's trade journals were saying, "Dairy Mart is sitting pretty by comparison" and "Dairy Mart is now absorbing a new 137-store acquisition and reporting strong earnings growth."

No question about it, we were unique. We're the only large convenience store chain that wasn't in bankruptcy by 1992 and we've flourished since the Braxton Report came out.

It doesn't take a rocket scientist to understand why those others got in trouble. In May, 1990, the Circle K chain went into bankruptcy because it was apparently paying too much for the stores it was buying. There were times Circle K paid $350,000 per store as contrasted with our average of paying around $50,000 per store.

Most of the money for buying stores is borrowed and the more you pay, the more you borrow, and the higher the interest payment, the more the store has to earn. So, when Circle K paid almost SEVEN TIMES as much as we did for a store, that meant it had to pay at least seven times as much in interest.

My dear friends, Stan and Dick, at Convenient Food Marts went into bankruptcy for other reasons. Perhaps one reason was that we had been their biggest regional franchisee, and they were in the midst of a lawsuit over the use of the alleged tradename "Convenient," the plaintiff claiming it was a generic name and not something they could trademark and copyright. The court agreed. Around this time, we and two other regional franchisees terminated our franchise agreements. That cost Stan and Dick about $1 million a year in franchise fees and that loss hurt them.

> *Too many people look at the top two and judge the industry by the top two. [Both Circle K and 7-Eleven are in Chapter 11 bankruptcy.] With National Convenient Stores in Chapter 11 and Cumberland Farms having just filed Chapter 11, people are saying, "God, this industry is going down the tubes."*
>
> *If you really look at all the companies that filed Chapter 11, they had too much leverage, too much debt to pay. 7-Eleven's average debt, if you divide by the number of stores, it was $450,000 per store. Circle K, $280,000 per store. Take a look at Dairy Mart, $50,000 per store. Quite a big difference.*
>
> —Frank Colaccino

The other important factor giving Dairy Mart long-term stability was to keep a solid management team in place. We were, after all, a company whose stock is traded on the NASDAQ national exchange with sales approaching one BILLION dollars!

In the fall of 1987 as I was getting close to my 65th birthday, I had a meeting of my Executive Committee, Larry Handler, Mitch Kupperman, Steve Montgomery and Frank Colaccino. I told them that I was nearing 65 and felt I shouldn't be Chief

Operating Officer any longer. That's when I said, "I'm going to appoint a new President. It's going to be one of you."

Then, like a father vainly trying to ensure continued harmony in the family after he's gone, "Now, I'd like a commitment from each of you that, whomever I pick as President, the other three are going to support him and you'll stay on board."

I don't remember who spoke up after a moment or two of silence, but whoever it was said, "Well, we will, but we're not sure for how long."

I guess, deep down, I really knew it was too much to ask the team to stay together once one of them was chosen President. Later, I would tell them when they pushed me for a decision,

"Fine, I will make that decision, but all four of you should understand that the one who becomes President must be strong enough to get along without the other three."

Again, they thought I was crazy, but I knew that the new President would want his own top-management team. The four knew how to work with me, but they may not be comfortable working with the new President. Besides, the new President had to have his own people. He was entitled to that and it was necessary for the future of the company. In other words, I had to give him a free-hand to function along with the title.

Actually, it is a basic rule of good management. You cannot give someone duties without the power to carry out those duties. With responsibility must go authority or the whole exercise is meaningless. I personally liked all four men, so liking them wasn't a factor. It came down to who was the best man for the job.

I decided on the man who was a bit of a maverick, who had the broadest experience in the business and who had enthusiasm for Dairy Mart. Emerson said nothing great was ever achieved without enthusiasm and that has been my creed. So, I looked for a man who, in all honesty, most closely resembled the image of myself.

I asked Frank to have dinner with me one night in October of 1988, but this in itself was not unusual. A nice dinner away from the office often serves many purposes, but Frank had no idea of the purpose of dinner that particular night until we came to coffee. I wanted it to be a special moment in his life.

I leaned back and said,

"Frank, I've got something to tell you. I've got something important to tell you. You are going to be the next President of Dairy Mart."

I made the mistake of saying this just as he picked up his cup of coffee and he almost spilled it all over himself.

At that point, he literally burst with enthusiasm. I have never liked executives who are too bland or blase about their jobs or their company and Frank didn't disappoint me that night. I had always been enthused about the company and was glad to know that I would be turning the reins over to someone who had my enthusiasm. Frank's enthusiasm reinforced my choice for the man who would take over my job someday.

After 20 minutes of talking about his future, I warned Frank of some of the problems ahead.

"You are going to have a difficult decision to make with Steve Montgomery. He has the largest block of stores in the company and they are in trouble. I also believe that Steve will have great difficulty accepting you as President of the total company."

"Now, it is your call to make, but I really think that you should make your headquarters, as head of the entire company, in Ohio. You know the Southeast Division because you've been there and you know the Northeast Division pretty well, and it is not that big, but you don't know our largest division out in the Midwest.

"You can function as President of the Midwest Division and of the entire company at the same time and do it best in Ohio."

"Gee, I'd like to see Steve succeed. Maybe I can help him."

"I would like to see him succeed, too. I hope you can make it work, but I was just giving you some advice as I will do from time to time, but you don't have to take it. You will be calling the shots. You will be the President, but don't forget, the buck stops at the President's desk."

"Give me until next April and let me try a few things and then make up my mind at that time."

Of course, that was fine with me. I knew I would have to give Frank freedom to make both the right decisions and the wrong decisions. It is all part of becoming a seasoned chief executive officer.

Later, when I announced Frank as the new President, Larry

Handler made it clear he was hurt because he thought it should have been him. Steve Montgomery let me know he was disappointed because he had been sure the job was going to be his. It might have been if he'd shown a little more interest in the job he had, running the Midwest Division. He had personality by the ton, but after Frank became President, he lost his steam when it came to our business.

When Walter Chrysler started building automobiles someone asked him why he felt his company was selling so many cars: "Well," he said, "I am an engineer and I don't know much about salesmanship, but one thing I have noticed is that the salesman who sells the most cars is the one who is all steamed up about Chrysler cars. So I tell all of my dealers to only hire salesmen who are exploding with enthusiasm over our cars."

That's how it worked out with Steve and Larry, and I was genuinely sorry that they didn't make it across the finish line. They weren't willing to stay on after I made my decision. Soon, both Steve and Larry were gone. Each got a year's severance, the ability to exercise stock options and their company cars. They were replaced by talented men who were aggressive and enthusiastic, Bob Stein for Steve and Greg Landry for Larry. Frank needed to be able to have his own team!

Frank picked Greg Landry, the financial man he had trained and had done such good work with Frank in the CONNA operation.

At my suggestion, Frank selected Bob Stein to fill Steve Montgomery's shoes. I had a good sense of Bob from my previous relationships with him.

Bob had been number two man to Larry Handler in the financial department and was an aggressive kind of guy who got things done. He was a real pusher.

However, sometimes he pushed in the wrong way. For example, he came into my office one day and presented me with a report and proceeded to tell me that I should do this, this and this. And I said, "Bob, you are in the finance department. Is that right?" He said, "Yeah." So I continued, "Well when you come in with a financial report, you give me the numbers. Then I am the one who makes the operating decisions. Don't you start telling me what I am going to do."

He didn't understand that and he got mad and didn't speak

to me for the better part of a month. Then he stuck his head in the door one day and said, "I can't stand this any longer. I gotta talk with you." I said, "Fine, come on in and sit down." He said, "What did I do wrong?"

"Bob, I don't think you listened very well the first time I explained it to you, but I'll try again," was the way I started. "You cannot, as an executive, allow your finance people, no matter how good their intentions, to make your operating decisions for you. In the finance department, you people work up the figures. Then you give them to me. I study them. Then I make the necessary operating decisions. If I do not understand your figures, I may call on you to explain them to me. But unless I specifically ask for your comments or recommendations, just prepare and present your figures. If you want to be an executive making operating decisions, I must tell you that the finance department is not the place for you."

It was just two weeks after our conversation when Frank called me and told me that Steve Montgomery would no longer be working for us, and I suggested that he consider Bob Stein for his replacement. Frank said that Bob would be fine with him because he, too, was thinking of him as Steve's replacement.

So I brought Bob Stein into my office and said, "Do you remember the lesson you learned about the difference between someone in finance preparing reports and the executive you submit the reports to making the operating decisions?" Of course, he remembered and I continued with, "Let me tell you something. You are going into a different position with this company. You are about to become General Manager of our Midwest Division. When you get to Ohio, people in finance will be handing you reports. You will study them carefully. And guess what? You will then make a decision. And don't you ever let your finance people tell you the decision to make."

If the lesson had not been clear before, it was cleared up that day, and I must say that Bob Stein has done a tremendous job of making decisions as head of the Midwest Division. He has made that operation flourish. From the day he went there, things started to improve. He has increased the margin of profit and is well thought of within the company.

So, now Dairy Mart has survived as a strong convenience

store chain in spite of the Braxton Report and failures of other chains. It has a strong, young team at the helm that I believe will guide it to continued success by being flexible and responsive to the changing profile of the convenience store industry.

Since my team of key executives—Frank Colaccino, Mitch Kupperman, Greg Landry and Bob Stein—had worked so hard to help make my dream come true, I decided the time had come for them take control of the company. So, on March 16, 1992, a partnership group headed by Frank Colaccino and including the other three acquired controlling interest of Diary Mart Convenience Stores. I remain Chairman of the Board and a substantial limited partner together with HNB Investments of New York City, but the company is now truly theirs to run.

My management team has put their money where their mouth is. They felt they were ready to take over. I felt they were ready to take over. And, with Frank's untiring efforts, he convinced HNB, and the Connecticut Development Authority and me that he and his team should take over. It is a young team. A strong team. A team dedicated to making Dairy Mart grow and prosper during the years ahead.

I am very pleased to see these young men commit themselves to the future of the company my wife and I worked so hard to build. It is in good hands now and it is a good feeling to know this.

I predict that this team under the leadership of Frank Colaccino will reach goals and do things that far exceed any of the goals and marks I have ever made. As a substantial equity holder, I am very pleased to have this dynamic management team lead Dairy Mart into the 21st Century. I believe we have made a positive move that will see this young management team take Dairy Mart to new heights.

I would like to quote just briefly from what the new President and Chief Executive Officer of Dairy Mart, Frank Colaccino, had to say in his message to the stockholders in the Company's annual report for the 1992 fiscal year.

"We will continue to look abroad for business opportunities in the global marketplace. As a successful convenience store chain in the United States, we have knowledge and expertise which people seek in other parts of the world. Our South Korean licensee has grown to become the largest convenience store chain in that country, with 58 stores at this writing. Additionally, Dairy Mart is on the verge of entering into a new joint venture to develop convenience store operations in Mexico, marking our first entry into Latin America. We expect our Mexican venture to be an early earnings contributor, as our Asian and Western European arrangements already have been."

So here we have a team with a leader, Frank Colaccino, who has a vigorous and powerful plan for the future. I am confident that the future will be theirs.

It has been a long time since I was hawking ice cream from a peddler's box and Jan and I were loading trucks and working out of a car that was our office.

Along the way I have learned the benefits of love, loyalty, and labor. I have learned to accept adversity and move on and I have learned that *determination* and *persistence* are the twin secrets to success. I saw both of these myself repeatedly, as well as in the life of my mother.

As Jimmy Stewart put it in the movie that is shown each year about Christmas time, "It's a Wonderful Life." It truly is. Thanks to a lot of wonderful people!

EPILOGUE

Our lives turn on tiny pivots and mine turned on the hope that bloomed in my mother's heart that day in 1912 when my father received the letter from his brother, Charles, in America. That hope, nurtured by her determination to do whatever had to be done for her family's survival and happiness, made this story possible.

As I said at the beginning of this very private story, if my mother's will had not prevailed in getting her family out of Koretz in the Russian Ukraine, neither I nor my children nor the Dairy Mart company or anything else I have achieved would exist.

I know because my wife, Jan, and I visited Koretz a few years ago. Of the 6,000 Jews living there at the time my father left for America, there were only two left. Neither of them were

Nirenbergs. All the others were slaughtered by the Russians, Poles or Germans or driven out.

She is gone now, but to this day I bless my mother and her unconquerable spirit which is still with me.